FINDING FREEDOM
IN CHRIST

Breakthrough

A STUDY IN GALATIANS

BARB ROOSE

Abingdon Women/Nashville

Breakthrough

Finding Freedom in Christ

ISBN 978-1-7910-1422-3

21 22 23 24 25 26 27 28 29 30 — 10 9 8 7 6 5 4 3 2 1

MANUFACTURED IN THE UNITED STATES OF AMERICA

Contents

About the Author

Barb Roose is a popular speaker and author who is passionate about teaching women to live beautifully strong and courageous in spite of their fears so that they can experience God's great adventure of faith and purpose for their lives. Barb enjoys teaching and encouraging women at conferences and events across the country, as well as internationally. She is the author of the Bible studies *Breakthrough: Finding Freedom in Christ*, *Surrendered: Letting Go and Living Like Jesus*, *I'm Waiting God: Finding Blessing in God's Delays*, *Joshua: Winning the Worry Battle*, and *Beautiful Already: Reclaiming God's Perspective on Beauty* and the books *Surrendered: 40 Devotions to Help You Let Go and Live Like Jesus*, *Winning the Worry Battle: Life Lessons from the Book of Joshua*, and *Enough Already: Winning Your Ugly Struggle with Beauty*. She also writes a regular blog at BarbRoose.com and hosts the *Better Together* podcast. Previously Barb was executive director of ministry at CedarCreek Church in Perrysburg, Ohio, where she served on staff for fourteen years and co-led the annual Fabulous Women's Conference that reached more than ten thousand women over five years. Barb is the proud mother of three adult daughters and lives in Northwest Ohio.

Follow Barb:

   @barbroose

   @barbroose

   Facebook.com/barbararoose

Blog   BarbRoose.com
(check here for event dates and booking information)

Introduction

Have you ever felt like there's a long list of rules you have to follow in order to be a "good Christian," and you always seem to be breaking one of them? Perhaps you feel like you're just one mistake or sin away from God sending you a big "whammy." Or maybe you're just tired of trying to measure up. Whether you grew up in church and were there every time the doors were open, attended church only on Christmas and Easter, or never darkened the door of a church until recently, you might be able to relate to one or more of those feelings. The truth is, many of us have been shaped by the idea that in order to please God, we've got to jump through religious hoops—what I call the To-Do, Do-More, and Do-Better hoops. So if that's you, you're not alone!

I grew up in church. My grandfather sat in the front row of our little black Baptist church, and as a deacon, he prayed with a low, booming voice every week. My grandmother played piano for the choir while my mom and aunts clapped and sang. In the early 80's, men still wore suits and hats to church while my grandmother and her friends wore fancy two-piece dress suits and fabulous hats. Back then, my grandmother and her friends anchored those fancy embellished hats with a legion of bobby pins in case they felt like jumping up and down as the gospel music started "getting good." Later I learned an important secret: My grandma and her friends didn't style their hair underneath their hats! In time, those hats became a symbol for the kind of Christianity I witnessed and lived much of my life: *Your life might be a mess on the inside, but as long as you look good on the outside, that's all people care about.*

From my earliest memories, I learned the "do's" and "don't's" each week at church. Don't run. Sit still and don't draw in the hymnbook. One rule still perplexes me today: If you need to leave the service to go to the restroom, signal that you're leaving and plan to come back by pointing your index finger in the air as you slip out of the sanctuary quietly. No doubt you can name your own perplexing rules.

As a kid, I was taught that God sent Jesus to die for my sins so that I could go to heaven. I loved the idea of heaven. Yet, at the same time, I worried that God might strike me dead for making a mistake. For many years, I followed Jesus more out of fear than faith. The result was that I cared more about aligning my beliefs and behaviors with the rules I learned by watching people on Sunday rather than concentrating on God's Word and learning what it means to have a relationship with God.

For a long time, I thought that following my rules-driven Christianity is why I had a good family, didn't get sick often, and did well in school. But when I went away to college, the day came when I tired of following the rules. I didn't want to jump through religious hoops anymore; I wanted to run wild and free. So, I abandoned the rules, which for me felt like abandoning what I called my faith.

When I eventually messed up my life so badly that there was nothing I could do to fix it, I experienced an ah-ha moment that changed my life: *God's love for me is based on His perfect promises, not my performance.* Whether that's a new concept for you or you've known it for years yet still struggle to live by it, this study will help you to stop jumping through hoops and embrace the life-changing freedom of the gospel of grace.

In his letter to a church that was overrun with people who wanted to be the rules-police, a pastor named Paul poured out his heart and faith to set the people straight. His letter to the Galatians touches on so many of the same questions, tensions, and problems that we still face today:

- What is freedom in Christ? (Galatians 2:4)
- Who has led us to believe that we have to keep the law to be right with God? (Galatians 2:21; 3:1)
- Why do we think we have to try to be perfect for God? (Galatians 3:3)
- Do we have to follow rules to earn God's favor and blessing? (Galatians 3:5)
- Why were the rules given in the first place? (Galatians 3:19)
- How do we live as one in Christ when we're all so different? (Galatians 3:26)
- How do we stay free in Christ? (Galatians 5:1)
- How do we use our freedom to make a difference? (Galatians 6:9)

If you've ever struggled with any of these questions or felt trapped by rules or religion, this study will provide a path for you to discover your freedom in Christ.

Getting Started

Each week there are five lessons combining study of Scripture with reflection and application. In addition to the study content, you'll find a daily Big Idea, Extra Insights, a weekly Memory Verse, and a weekly Breakthrough Reflection Exercise.

Much of the *Breakthrough* study experience will come with your commitment to make space and quiet time to let the Holy Spirit speak to your heart. Breakthroughs cannot be planned or forced, but they can be experienced by regular, intentional time with God.

In this six-week study, you'll be encouraged to embrace the following six Freedom Principles:

FREEDOM PRINCIPLES
1. The gospel is based on God's perfect promises, not our performance.
2. A relationship with God means that we receive *from* Him rather than follow rules *for* Him.
3. Your freedom in Christ cannot be shaken or taken away by anyone who chooses not to live like Christ.
4. Freedom in Christ is living free from fear and fully alive with joy and purpose.
5. Spiritual breakthrough is an ah-ha moment when we recognize that God is at work within us, receive what He's doing, and respond to it.
6. You are God's beautiful, lovable, capable daughter. You are confident in Christ and worthy of God's best.

Each daily lesson should take about twenty to thirty minutes. You'll need a Bible, a pen, and an open heart that is ready to receive whatever God might speak or reveal—which could be the first step, next step, or even the breakthrough step for you. These lessons will prepare you for the discussion and activities of your weekly session, if you're meeting in a group.

Though you can do the study on your own and reap benefits, *Breakthrough* is designed to be done with a group for encouragement, support, and accountability. As you gather together in person or virtually to watch the *Breakthrough* videos, you will have the opportunity to share what you are learning and to pray together. Each video message is designed to follow and complement the content that you have studied during the week. Whether or not your group watches the video, it's so helpful to share your struggles and victories with each other. As you do, you'll encourage one another and find strength to complete the study and put into practice everything that you're learning.

A Final Word

Can I tell you just how happy that I am that you're taking this *Breakthrough* journey with me? It doesn't matter where you come from or what you've been through, you can know and trust that God is with you and for you. Wherever you need a breakthrough, God has already promised freedom and desires to give it to you. Finding freedom in Christ will not only bless and transform your own life; you'll be a shining light of God's hope and glory to the world around you!

Blessings,

Barb

Biblical Background on Galatians

The apostle Paul is accepted as the author of this letter to a group of New Testament churches in Galatia. His letter is considered among scholars to be one of the most significant books in the New Testament, second only to Romans. In fact, one scholar notes:

Galatians has been called the "Declaration of Independence of Christian liberty." The great reformer Martin Luther especially loved this letter; he called Galatians his "Catherine von Bora" after his wife, because, he said, "I am married to it."[1]

There are a number of themes in the Letter to the Galatians that help define its significance and influence:

- Freedom in Christ
- Justification/Righteousness

- Unity in Christ
- Living by the Spirit
- Life of Purpose

Map of Galatia During Paul's Time

Whenever I'm studying Scripture and the text makes numerous references to different places, that's a clue to me that I need to check out a map of the geography of that time. A map creates a sense of reality by helping us to visualize the physical location of the people in Scripture who lived long ago. As I point out in my study *Joshua: Winning the Worry Battle*, sometimes geographical areas can carry important lessons of their own, including spiritual symbolism that adds to the richness of God's revelation to us.

Here is a map showing the Roman province of Galatia (and surrounding areas) in Paul's time, which covered a large area located in modern-day Turkey. You'll notice that it stretches from the Black Sea in the north to the Mediterranean Sea in the south. This large geographical footprint of Galatia has created an ongoing debate about who Paul may have been writing to in his letter. (More on that below.) We do know that, as a part of Rome, Galatia had many different ethnic groups living within its borders.

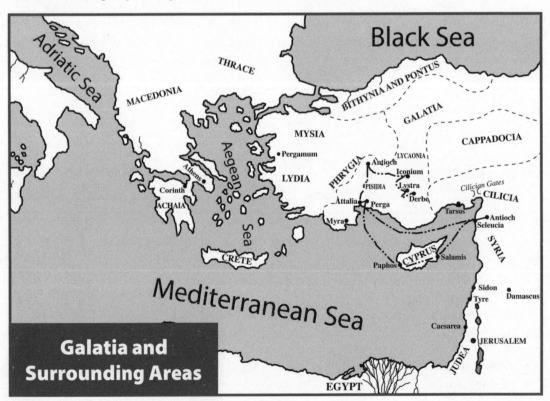

Take a moment to locate the cities of Antioch, Iconium, Lystra, and Derbe on the map. These are the cities in Southern Galatia where Paul and his companions planted churches during his first missionary journey as reported in Acts 16:6. The narrative report of their church planting efforts in Galatians are recorded in Acts 13 and 14. Paul made a great deal of personal sacrifice to plant those churches, so as we get into our study of Galatians and notice that he writes with a candid and confrontational tone, we can remember that he put his life on the line to bring the gospel to them.

Intrigue in the Background

While historical and biblical research points to Paul as the author of the letter to the Galatians, there is ongoing debate regarding the actual date of the letter and exactly where Paul directed his letter.[2] In fact, this scholarly debate is still unsettled. Following are the two theories proposed about Paul's literary timeline and direction.

1. *Southern Galatian Theory*. Scholars who advocate the southern Galatian theory propose that Paul wrote the letter to the churches in southern Galatia around AD 49 after his first missionary journey.[3] They use Acts 13 and 14 as one of the pillars to support their position. Scholars supporting this theory also point out that Paul makes specific reference to planting the churches in the southern region but does not cite specific cities in the northern region. There could be many reasons for this, so a lack of mention may or may not mean anything.[4]
2. *Northern Galatian Theory*. Scholars who support this theory say that Paul's letter was addressed to the believers in the northern areas of Galatia.[5] One scholar argued that Paul wouldn't have used the term "Galatians" to describe the people who lived in the southern area of Galatia because of their ethnic background. Supporters of the northern theory date Paul's letter around AD 50-57.[6]

This brief summary is a high-level explanation of a very in-depth debate. Here's a conclusion from one scholar:

We must admit that untangling the knots in deciphering the destination of Galatians is difficult. . . . Identifying the recipients of Galatians is important for Pauline chronology and history, but it is not determinative for the interpretation of the letter, and the meaning of the letter does not change dramatically whether we opt for a north or south Galatian hypothesis.[7]

The bottom line is that the debate regarding timeline and direction (recipients) has zero impact on the validity and credibility of Paul's message.

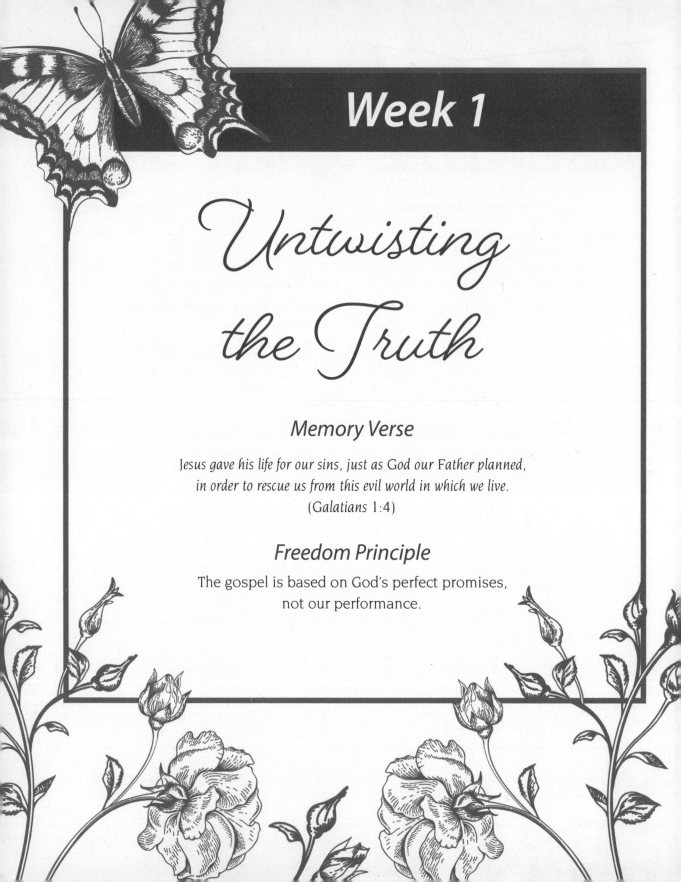

Week 1

Untwisting the Truth

Memory Verse

*Jesus gave his life for our sins, just as God our Father planned,
in order to rescue us from this evil world in which we live.*
(Galatians 1:4)

Freedom Principle

The gospel is based on God's perfect promises,
not our performance.

Paul begins his letter to the Galatians by saying that Jesus has the power to rescue or free us from this evil world (Galatians 1:4). This was the "leading news" about Jesus after His resurrection. But even during Jesus's ministry, there was much talk among the people about His amazing power.

Imagine the whispers among Jesus's old friends and neighbors when He arrived back in his hometown of Nazareth after beginning His ministry. He used to be a carpenter or builder, but something had changed. The people heard rumors from Galilee about Jesus (Luke 4:14-15), and now that He was back for a visit, they no doubt were curious.

I recall a time years ago when someone I knew won a popular reality television show. When this person arrived at a class reunion the next year, there were a lot of behind-the-hand whispers. People wondered if this person had changed and, if so, what was different. This kind of curiosity is part of our human nature.

On the Sabbath, Jesus entered His hometown synagogue along with the others in the community. The service opened as usual with several blessings and various readings from the Torah and the prophets, followed by a short sermon or message.[1]

As the men sat in the front and the women sat separately in the back, Jesus stood before the people who had watched him grow up and began to read from the scroll of the prophet Isaiah that was handed to Him:

> [18]"*The Spirit of the LORD is upon me,*
> > *for he has **anointed me to bring Good News** to the poor.*
> *He has sent me to proclaim **that captives will be released**,*
> > *that the blind will see,*
> **that the oppressed will be set free,**
> > [19]*and that the time of the LORD's favor has come.*"
> > > (Luke 4:18-19, emphasis added)

This prophetic passage written centuries earlier told of the Messiah who would bring salvation to the Jews. As the audience heard phrases such as "bring Good News," "captives . . . released," and "the oppressed . . . set free," perhaps their thoughts focused on freedom from Roman rule and restoration to full sovereignty as a nation.

At first, the audience seemed to be proud of their hometown son, even though they were puzzled by Jesus's proclamation: "The Scripture you've just heard has been fulfilled this very day!" (Luke 4:21). As they were questioning with amazement all that they had heard, Jesus continued speaking, saying that no prophet is accepted in his own hometown and suggesting that perhaps that was why Elijah and Elisha ministered to foreigners instead of their own people (Luke 4:23-27).

Wait...what? Jaws would have dropped. Furious whispers would have flown around the room. In one breath, Jesus suggested that He had the power to set them free, and in another He basically implied that their unbelief would not allow Him to do so. No doubt the crowd began grumbling, "Who does Jesus think He is?" In fact, they mobbed Him and tried to throw Him off a cliff (Luke 4:28-29).

Regardless of what the people believed about Jesus, He *did* have the power to set them free—and that's exactly what He came to do. A short time later, Jesus paid the ultimate price so that we all could be free. Jesus conquered sin and death, delivering us from their power, so we might live in freedom and experience God's great adventure of faith and purpose for our lives.

This is the gospel that Paul writes about in his letter to the Galatians. We begin our study this week by defining this gospel and how it brings freedom into our lives. Then I will continue to illuminate the specific ways we've been set free in Christ and how we can live in that freedom.

If you're questioning whether or not the gospel's power is strong enough to set you free, let me assure you that it is! If you're afraid that the gospel can't deliver you from the fear that you aren't good enough for God on your own, I'm confident it can! I believe it because I have experienced it. Jesus came, died, and rose again to rescue you and me from *whatever* it is that keeps us from experiencing freedom. So, let's begin!

Day 1: The Gospel: God's Rescue and Our Release

Big Idea

The gospel is for *all* of us, no matter where we've come from or what we've done.

There was some confusion among the Galatian believers over some important matters, and the apostle Paul wrote a letter to bring clarification and understanding. At the core of the confusion simmered this question: *What is the gospel?*

As the founding pastor of the churches in Galatia, Paul had preached the gospel and established the churches in that area. He had told them all about how Jesus came to set them free from the penalty of sin and death. And as the Holy Spirit had moved in the hearts of the people, they had said "yes" to God's offer of forgiveness.

Then came troubling news. Paul heard reports that the Galatian believers were saying and doing things in conflict with the truth of the gospel. Not only that, but a group of people in the church championed a different version

of the gospel than what Paul taught. Unfortunately, that group was gaining influence, and their message was beginning to distract and divide the church.

Even today there are times when personal agendas or false versions of the gospel distract or divide the church. When this happens, people get hurt. In fact, there's a term called "church hurt," which refers to the emotional, spiritual, or abusive wounds that someone experiences within a Christian community. If this has ever happened to you, let me say that your "church hurt" hurts the heart of God. Tomorrow, we're going to examine the gospel in more depth, but I want to say this right now: though it requires sacrifice and surrender, the true gospel never hurts or manipulates anyone.

At the beginning of his letter, Paul establishes his credibility with the Galatian church. As a leader, he is mission-driven by the gospel message and nothing else. (This is an excellent example for all of us to follow wherever we have influence in our churches. It's easy to allow other agendas to distract and divide the church, so we must center ourselves around the gospel and nothing else.) Take a look for yourself.

Read Galatians 1:1. How does Paul identify himself?

Who appointed Paul as an apostle?

Paul has credibility and a powerful source of authority in his role as apostle because Jesus Himself divinely appointed Paul for the job. According to tradition, Paul authored thirteen of the books in the New Testament, although some scholars today debate his authorship of several books.[2] As he wrote to various churches throughout his ministry, Paul began most of his letters by establishing his credibility as an apostle of Christ (Romans 1:1, 1 Corinthians 1:1, Ephesians 1:1, Colossians 1:1). Perhaps he knew that people would talk about his past and question his right to lead and teach them.

Read Galatians 1:2. To whom is Paul's letter addressed?

_____ a single church   _____ multiple churches in Galatia

In the Biblical Background on Galatians (pages 9-12), we read about the ongoing scholarly debate regarding when Paul wrote this letter and where it was directed—to the churches in Northern or Southern Galatia. Much of the research leans toward the perspective that Paul wrote to the believers

Extra Insight

An apostle is "a special messenger of Jesus Christ; a person to whom Jesus delegated authority for certain tasks...The word 'apostle' has a wider meaning in the letters of the apostle Paul. It includes people who, like himself, were not included in the Twelve but who saw the risen Christ and were specially commissioned by Him."[3] (See Acts 1:21-22; 2:32; and 3:15.)

in Southern Galatia, having planted a number of churches in various cities there. In Acts 16, we learn that Paul and Barnabas traveled throughout the area, not only sharing the gospel but also establishing local churches in cities such as Derbe, Lystra, and Iconium. However, evangelism ain't easy! In his travels, Paul encountered some pretty dramatic events such as being mistaken for a deity, having the crowd throw stones at him, being confronted by angry religious people, and more (see Act 14:8-20).

Once we read about everything that Paul and Barnabas escaped, endured, or suffered, we understand more about why Paul cared so deeply about writing to the Galatians. He had a personal stake in sharing and clarifying the gospel because he had already sacrificed his health and welfare for them in the name of Christ. Though he had spent many years of his life punishing people for their faith in Christ, Paul willingly allowed punishment in his own life in order for Jesus's name to be proclaimed.

Read Galatians 1:11-14.

Who revealed the gospel to Paul?

What did Paul do before encountering Christ?

Once upon a time, Paul hunted down people who believed in Jesus, also known as followers of The Way. In verses 13-14, Paul describes how he violently persecuted the church. Other Scripture references detail Paul, also known as as Saul, entering homes and "dragging out both men and women to throw them into prison" (Acts 8:3). One day, Paul encountered Jesus while traveling on the road (Acts 9). It was during Jesus's confrontation with Saul that Jesus cast a new vision for his life. In Galatians 1:17-19, Paul explains that after his encounter with Christ, he traveled to Arabia and Damascus before eventually going to Jerusalem to meet with Peter.

However, Paul's past and his qualifications would be brought into question over and over again. Paul's enemies argued that he couldn't be an apostle because he wasn't a part of the original group of disciples. Yet, Paul didn't allow the accusations and doubt of others to keep him from living out Jesus's commands. "He was commissioned and taught *directly by the risen Jesus Himself.*"[4]

Read 1 Corinthians 15:9-10. How does Paul describe himself in relation to the other apostles?

In verse 9, what does Paul reveal about his past?

In verse 10 (NASB, NIV, NKJV, NRSV), Paul uses the same phrase twice. Fill in the blanks:

By the _____ of _____.

Paul's confidence to teach and preach boldly was fueled by living in God's grace for his life. As a powerful influence in the church, Paul stayed singularly focused on the gospel, which is a sharp contrast to the agenda of the troublemakers that we'll learn about later. Even though Paul heard about the voices of opposition that were planting doubt in the minds of the people, he remained faithful to what God had called him to do.

As in Paul's day, people throughout the centuries have tried to use the gospel for their personal agenda or gain. Paul's example provides a filter that we can use to discern whether or not someone is gospel-driven or agenda-driven. And like Paul, we too, can choose to remain faithful to the gospel despite what others do or say—including about us.

Paul didn't hide from or behind his past. He could have been ashamed of who he was, but instead he allowed the power of the gospel to rescue, restore, and redeem where he'd come from and what he'd done. This is the power of the gospel that is promised for all of us.

Jesus proclaimed that He had the power to set people free. Where do you feel like you've been stuck or struggling in your Christian life? Are there any places where you feel guilty or afraid you are disappointing God? Explain.

Are there any reasons you feel unqualified to be used by God? If so, list them here:

Do you have "church hurt" or a bad church experience from your past that is keeping you from trusting other Christians or participating in a local church? If so, describe it below:

It's okay if you couldn't answer some of those questions because they made you feel a little vulnerable. We're making this journey together, but we all bring our own experiences, needs, and desires. You have the freedom and grace to do what you can along the way, though I encourage you to circle back and fill in any unanswered questions at a later date. I'm thankful to be on the journey with you!

Prayer

God, I want to experience freedom in every area of my life. I choose to believe that if You can transform Paul's life, You can transform mine; too, in Jesus's name. Amen.

Day 2: The Gospel of Grace

Big Idea

The gospel changes everything about our lives every single day!

Have you ever heard about the *curse of knowledge*? This is when someone wrongly assumes that his or her audience knows the background or basic information to understand a situation or concept.[5] When my girls were in middle school and high school, I'd call or text them while I was at work and ask them to make a certain dish for dinner. I figured that since I'd made the dish at least fifty times while they watched, then they would know how to make it themselves. Except they didn't. I hadn't specifically trained or instructed them sufficiently for them to know what to do.

When it comes to understanding the gospel, the apostle Paul was careful to avoid the curse of knowledge with his audience. While there might have been believers who would have said, "Com'on Paul, I've heard all of this before," Paul still started from square one in his letter to the Galatians because the gospel is so often misinterpreted, misused, or misunderstood.

We're going to start from square one with the gospel today. God can bring fresh insight into our lives even through a verse or concept that we've studied many times before. Even if we've heard the gospel 1,000 times, we still need to hear it 1,000 times more, because the gospel changes everything about our lives every single day!

In Galatians 1:3, what does Paul pray that God gives the people? Fill in the blanks:

G _____ and P_____

Paul uses the phrase "grace and peace" several times in his letters to different audiences (Romans 1:7; 1 Corinthians 1:3; 2 Corinthians 1:2). This beautiful phrase captures his dream for the believers in Galatia: for them to live in God's grace and peace as they faced various areas of stress and strain, including adjusting to a new faith and withstanding the pressure applied by troublemakers. We'll consider the specifics of their circumstances later.

Extra Insight

Grace (*charis*) – God's kindness or favor[6]

Peace (*eirene*) – Quietness of mind, wholeness[7]

GRACE QUOTES

"These two terms, grace and peace, constitute Christianity."
—Martin Luther[8]

"Grace does not depend on what we have done for God but rather what God has done for us. Ask people what they must do to get to heaven and most reply, "Be good." Jesus's stories contradict that answer. All we must do is cry, "Help!"

—Philip Yancey[9]

"Your worst days are never so bad that you are beyond the *reach* of God's grace. And your best days are never so good that you are beyond the *need* of God's grace."

—Jerry Bridges[10]

Paul writes a brief summary of the gospel in Galatians 1:4. Write that verse in the space below:

In exchange for giving His life, what did Jesus's sacrifice do for us?

Galatians 1:3-4 captures an essential element of the gospel, which one scholar summarizes this way:

The good news [gospel] is that God became man and lived a perfect life that He might die on the cross for our sins and be raised from the dead in victory over sin so that all who believe in Him will be saved, not based on anything they have done, but based solely on what He has done.[11]

In the space below, write the gospel of grace message in your own words:

Extra Insight

"Only one-third of American adults (35 %) continue to embrace the traditional biblical view that salvation comes through the sacrifice of Jesus Christ."[13]

Gospel comes from the Greek word *euaggelion*, meaning "good news."[12] The gospel is God's rescue of humanity as we willingly surrender our lives to Him so that He can renew us, redeem our mistakes, and restore us to wholeness. At the core of the gospel is God's desire to give and our willingness to receive.

When I consider the message of the good news, I see that we receive God's grace, which means His kindness and favor. So throughout our study, I will periodically refer to the gospel as the *gospel of grace*.

Read the Scriptures and summarize in the space provided the main message of each verse:

"For this is how God loved the world: He gave his one and only Son, so that everyone who believes in him will not perish but have eternal life."

(John 3:16)

Summarize the verse:

For everyone has sinned; we all fall short of God's glorious standard.

(Romans 3:23)

Summarize the verse:

For the wages of sin is death, but the free gift of God is eternal life through Christ Jesus our Lord.

(Romans 6:23)

Summarize the verse:

This means that anyone who belongs to Christ has become a new person. The old life is gone; a new life has begun!
(2 Corinthians 5:17)

Summarize the verse:

For we are God's masterpiece. He has created us anew in Christ Jesus, so we can do the good things he planned for us long ago.
(Ephesians 2:10)

Summarize the verse:

As we allow God to love us, save us, change us, and give us purpose, the gospel positions us to experience God's great adventure for our lives. In one of Jesus's final messages to His disciples, He commanded them to go into the world and share the gospel (Matthew 28:19-20). This command also applies to us today. In my own life, God's great adventure of faith and purpose has included making ten overseas missions trips where I helped build homes and spoke at women's conferences through an interpreter. Other adventures have included leaving not one but two successful careers to take risks in ministry. Not every adventure has been easy. By definition, adventure also can include the unknown, like the years that our family sought help to navigate a difficult addiction crisis. All of these adventures, good and bad, came in response to the impact of the gospel on my life.

> **What situations in your life (past or present) demonstrate the adventures that the gospel has brought into your life?**

The image on the following page conveys a picture of the gospel message. The verses that you looked up earlier align with this gospel message.

Extra Insight

Adventure:
an undertaking usually involving danger and unknown risks; the encountering of risks; an exciting or remarkable experience.[14]

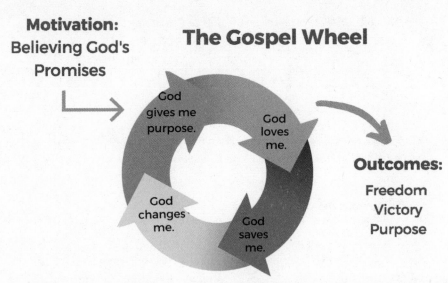

Motivation:
Believing God's
Promises

The Gospel Wheel

God gives me purpose.

God loves me.

God changes me.

God saves me.

Outcomes:

Freedom
Victory
Purpose

Notice that our part is to accept the gospel message and believe God's promises for our lives, but it is God's activity that drives the Gospel Wheel. He gives and He asks us to receive. As we dig into Paul's teaching to the Galatians, we will see that confusion erupted when the people stopped believing that receiving God's grace was enough to make them right with God, and they essentially created a to-do list in order to assure their salvation.

There are three essential elements for us to understand about the gospel. Let's review them together.

1. The gospel is based on God's perfect promises, not your performance.

At some point, we're all confronted with the uncomfortable feeling that the gospel is too good to be true for us. After all, we've seen our sin and shortcomings.

In Paul's letter to the believers in Galatia, you'll see his wholehearted embrace of God's grace and mercy. I love how one author describes God's heart toward us: "We do not deserve mercy, nor do we even know how to seek it. It seeks us. And it finds us. Mercy comes running, and by His grace, God pursues you with His love. His pleasure in you is not dependent on your pursuit of Him, but His pursuit of you."[15]

When you look at the Gospel Wheel, which aspect of God's activity is hardest for you to receive? Why?

2. You need the gospel each day of your life.

The gospel is just as true when you're screaming at another driver at a stop light or you've disconnected from your church because something painful happened to you there as it is the day you first accepted Jesus Christ into your life.

As you walk out your faith, you're still human. This is why we can't treat the gospel like the curse of knowledge in our lives, because each day we're still realizing the fullness of what it means to confront our sinful nature, acknowledge the price of our sin, and surrender our lives to Christ. If you've got this down, let me know!

> **Why do you need to remember the power of the gospel in your life *each day*?**

3. Watch out for anything that will poison your understanding of the gospel.

Authors David Platt and Tony Merida share the following analogy: "If you were about to drink a glass of clean water, and then someone added a drop of poison to it, would you still drink it? It's close to pure, right? No, it's totally contaminated and undrinkable as that drop of poison hits the water. It's the same way with the gospel."[16]

As the water illustration suggests, it takes very little to poison something pure. The gospel is pure, so once you start trying to do anything to earn or keep your salvation, it's no longer the gospel.

> **Is there anything you feel (or have felt) you must do to earn or keep your salvation? Explain.**

> **Our memory verse this week is Galatians 1:4. Read the verse through two times (page 12), and then fill in the blanks below:**
>
> *Jesus gave his _____ for our sins, just as God our Father planned, in order to _____ us from this evil world in which we live.*

Throughout our study, we're going to keep coming back to the gospel because that's the theme that Paul focuses on in his letter to the Galatians. Wherever we are in our understanding of the gospel, it's likely that at one time or another we've thought that we *must* earn our salvation or that we *can* earn our salvation. It is my prayer that by the end of our study, each of us will be sure that neither is true and will experience true freedom in Christ!

Prayer

Dear God, thank You for the gospel that saved my life! I am so grateful that You loved me enough to send Jesus to die for my sins. I couldn't save myself. In fact, I still can't save myself! Open my eyes and reveal any blind spots where I'm struggling to receive from You. I want to live each day in the beautiful fullness and freedom of what You've done for me; in Jesus's name. Amen.

Day 3: Untwisting the Truth

Big Idea

God wants more *for* you than *from* you.

Recently, I spoke with a young believer who feared that God would eventually tire of loving her. When I gently asked why she felt that way, she replied, "Well, because I still smoke, sometimes I forget to read my Bible, and when I look at other Christians, they seem to be doing everything better than me."

Oh, my heart hurt for this precious young woman! I sat in silence for a few beats and prayed. Prompted by the Holy Spirit, I whispered to her: *You can't mess up God's love for you.*

I don't know if you needed to hear that today, but I hope that you know deep in the innermost part of your soul that God loves you because of who He is and not because of anything that you've done. It is God's powerful love demonstrated through Christ that releases us from the feeling that we aren't enough for God, or from the people who make us believe that God wants more from us before He will fully love us.

Today's lesson is titled "Untwisting the Truth." The phrase "twist the truth" comes directly from Galaltians 1:7, which is part of the Scripture passage we're studying today. We'll see within the first few words of Paul's next statements that he's fully loaded with questions and challenges. He's furious about the lies the Galatian Christians have believed, but his heart is motivated by love for them. As we'll discover, Paul's not condemning or judging them; rather, he wants them to experience the kind of freedom that he has found in Christ. He wants to warn them about becoming twisted like the mistruths they're hearing.

What's twisted in your beliefs about God? The best way to know God's truth is to focus on His word rather than to fixate on the lies that are distracting you from the truth. As you look at Paul's teaching today, you'll be challenged to discover the distorted or perhaps even straight up wrong beliefs that you've been carrying around about God and how He sees you.

Read Galatians 1:6-9.

In verse 6, Paul expresses strong language about what the churches in Galatia are doing.

The people are turning away from _____.

They are following _____.

In verse 7, Paul tells the believers that they are being

_____.

Based on what you've read in this passage, what do you think Paul means in verse 7 when he uses the phrase "twist the truth"?

In verses 8-9, Paul declares a curse two times. Who will be cursed?

Extra Insight

Cursed is the Greek word *anathema*, which means "dedicated to destruction."[17]

Paul's distress is that the believers have turned away from the gospel. Rather than embrace the hope in Christ, the forgiveness of their sins, and the promise of eternal life, some Galatian believers dropped their connection to what they once believed. I've seen this happen over the years as various former Christian authors or artists have issued press releases proclaiming that after a time of enlightened self-reflection, they no longer consider them-selves Christians or no longer believe the Bible to be the Word of God. As a long-time staff member at my church, I also watched people come to church fired up in their new faith only to fade away over time for a variety of reasons. It's not for me to say what happened, but the end results seem to indicate that the gospel message had become twisted in some way.

It's important to note that there have been and always will be people who "stir the pot" in the church. Sometimes, it's a strong-willed individual who

Extra Insight

Council of Jerusalem

"A number of law-observant Jews are wondering why Paul and the church at Antioch are not insisting that the Gentile converts keep the law. The issue becomes divisive and threatens to split the movement. The wisest course of action is to convene a meeting with the leaders of the Jerusalem church and reach a mutual understanding that will govern the movement as more and more Gentiles put their faith in Christ."[19]

loves Jesus and also likes to tell the pastor how to do his or her job. Other times, it's a person or group of believers who express dissension regarding various church or denominational traditions. But sometimes it's a group of people like the one we are studying today—dangerous troublemakers with unholy agendas who cause confusion and distraction from the gospel.

After Paul and Barnabas came back to Antioch, which is located in southern Galatia, a group of people showed up and started teaching what Paul calls "a different kind of Good News" (Galatians 1:8). These people were known as Judaizers, or "early converts to Christianity who tried to force believers from non-Jewish backgrounds to adopt Jewish customs as a condition of salvation."[18] Paul not only says that these people were preaching a different kind of Good News; he says that their different Good News was not actually the Good News at all (Galatians 1:6-7).

Read Acts 15:1. What did the Judaizers tell the believers?

Read Philippians 3:2. According to this verse, how did Paul feel about them? What did he call them?

Acts 15 records the meeting of the Jerusalem Council held to discuss the Judaizers' argument, which was gaining traction. (For more about the Jerusalem Council, see the Extra Insight in the margin.) In Acts 15:5, it is revealed that the Judaizers were also Pharisees who were upset about how the Gentiles were being accepted into the church. The Judaizers wanted to add requirements to salvation, saying that "to be saved . . . one had to believe in Jesus and be circumcised."[20] Though we might think that Paul and the other Christians should have been able to simply say "no" to this and move on, the Judaizers gained tremendous influence.

According to one commentator, some of the motivation behind the Judaizers' insistence and the effectiveness of their message was that the law observers wanted to avoid persecution. He writes, "Their motivation for advocating circumcision was to escape persecution from Zealot radicals who were terrorizing Palestine. These Zealot revolutionaries were hostile to Christian Jews who tolerated fellowship with uncircumcised Gentiles."[21] There's some irony here because Paul used to be a Zealot, and now the Judaizers were preaching against this former Zealot who now wouldn't hurt them in order to avoid punishment from those who could. Yet Paul contended with his audience to hold on to the gospel message regardless of what others said.

What's an issue within your church or denomination that has created conflict?

How does this conflict impact how you feel when you're at church or trying to stay engaged in your faith?

If you've been a part of church for more than a few years, chances are you've seen some human-related shortcomings that hurt not only others but also the heart of God. However, the power of the gospel is and always will be greater than our human failings, which is exactly why we need the gospel!

The only way to "untwist the truth" about the gospel in our lives is to strategically and ruthlessly focus on the truth. Look up each verse, and write the truth(s) revealed about who God is and how He sees you.

Psalm 34:18-19

Jeremiah 31:3

Zephaniah 3:17

John 14:6

Romans 8:1

When you look at these truths that you've identified, which one or two stand out to you today? Why?

What aspects of who God is have you allowed to get twisted, either through your life experience or the influence of others?

What lies about yourself have you believed, either through your life experience or the influence of others?

Though we do not have control over how others behave, we always have control over who and what we choose to believe. Above all, we are to follow the message of the gospel and Christ's vision for the kingdom of God in our world. We can be honest about the people, problems, and pain that we've experienced in the church, but we must never use that to justify our disobedience to God or our failure to trust in His promises for our lives.

It's so easy for us to believe the lies instead of God's truth, but I pray that you allow the power of the verses you read today to untwist any lies that you've believed. God loves *you*.

Prayer

O, God, let me cling only to what is true! God, reveal to me any twisted truths I'm harboring in my head or heart about who You are or how You see me.

I've been holding on to a twisted truth that _____.

But the real truth is _____.

In light of Your real truth, I now choose to believe _____.

God, whenever I think that the gospel isn't enough for my faults and failures, remind me that, in fact, it is more than enough. Thank You for the gift of grace, which I cannot earn but need each day; in Jesus's name. Amen.

Day 4: The To-Do, Do-More, and Do-Better Hoops

Whether we were brought up in a religious environment or we've never darkened the doorstep of a church, many of us want to know what we need to do to make God happy so that we can get what we want from Him. Sometimes, those rules are given to us by religious authority figures, and other times we create our own list of rules that we think will fast-track us to God's blessing—or at least keep us out of God's hammer strike zone.

Yesterday, we were introduced to a group of people in the Galatian church who wanted to add requirements to salvation. These Judaizers gained enough influence to plant doubt into the minds of the believers. As a result, many Galatian Christians shifted from the posture of receiving from God to thinking that they needed to do something for God in order to be worthy of salvation. As a result, they unintentionally trapped themselves in a cycle of religious rules and robbed themselves of God's power, peace, and provision in their lives. The word that describes our human effort to gain God's favor is *legalism*.[22]

Legalism is when we focus on what we're doing for God rather than on what we're receiving from Him. This "doing" looks like religious rules we follow in hopes of earning God's favor. Legalism isn't always about tradition. It's not legalistic to go to church, but it *is* legalism to go to church if you think that church attendance earns you points with God. I make sure that I do my Bible study each day. This would be legalistic if I did my Bible study because I felt like it made me a better Christian. However, I do my Bible study because I want to stay as close to God as I can each day! That's definitely not legalism.

As we will continue to discover throughout this study, we have a lot in common with the Galatians. Today we'll learn about the three religious hoops of legalism and, most important, we'll learn a helpful filtering tool that we can use to determine whether our motives are driven by rules or by a desire to lean into our relationship with God.

Before Paul confronted the legalistic Judaizers, Jesus challenged the Pharisees, who also prioritized following rules over receiving from a relationship God.

Big Idea

A relationship with God means that you receive from Him rather than follow a bunch of rules.

Extra Insight

"U.S. adults today adopt a 'salvation-can-be-earned' perspective, with a near-majority (48%) believing that if a person is generally good, or does enough good things during their life, they will 'earn' a place in Heaven."[23]

Read Matthew 12:1-2, and fill in the blanks below.

Jesus and the disciples were walking in a grain field on the

_____.

The disciples were hungry, so they broke off some heads of grain to _____ them.

The Pharisees protested because they felt that the disciples violated the religious _____ about harvesting grain on the Sabbath.

And when you enter your neighbor's field of grain, you may pluck the heads of grain with your hand, but you must not harvest it with a sickle.

(Deuteronomy 23:25)

In next week's lessons, we will learn about the religious laws that the Pharisees and Judaizers wanted to enforce upon the Galatian believers. In this section of Scripture, Jesus's disciples were hungry, so they broke off some heads of grain from a farmer's field. This was an acceptable practice at the time (see Deuteronomy 23:25 in the margin)—though I can't resist saying that it is unacceptable to do this with grapes at the grocery store!

The Pharisees, who served as the moral and religious authority for the Jewish people, saw the disciples break off the grain. While they knew that it wasn't unlawful to pick grain by hand, they protested about doing it on the Sabbath. Like the Judaizers who would follow in their legalistic footsteps later, the Pharisees focused on following rules in order to be right with God. In their defense, these legalists thought that they were defending God.

Legalism leads us to believe that rules are the only way we can be assured we are right with God. When we believe there are rules that define what makes someone a good Christian versus a bad Christian, that's legalism. Some examples include rules about what we can or cannot eat, what music is good or bad for us to listen to, or what Bible translations we should read—all of which have nothing to do with receiving from God or enjoying a life-giving relationship with Him.

What are some religious rules that some Christians unintentionally pressure other Christians to follow?

What are some legalistic rules you've thought you had to live by—in the past or present?

Salvation is not a reward for the good things we have done, so none of us can boast about it.

(Ephesians 2:9)

Read Ephesians 2:9 in the margin, and summarize the message of this verse below:

While some legalism is motivated by not feeling we're enough for God, there's another kind of legalism that is driven by pride. When we think that God loves us because we've earned it, we're prone to boast or brag. A good example of this is the Pharisees, who felt that because they followed the law, they were better than other Jews. This kind of legalism assumes a quid pro quo with God. Q*uid pro quo* means we carry the expectation that if we do our part, then the other party should hold up their end of the bargain.

Again, the gospel is based on God's perfect promises, not our performance. Our relationship with God is about receiving from Him, not following a bunch of rules for Him. All rules do is discourage us and make us tired!

Legalism's rules tend to fall into three categories I've defined with three hoops labeled To Do, Do More, and Do Better.

To Do
An attempt to gain God's forgiveness or save one's self from sin or struggle

Do More
An effort to compel God to act or gain favor (like a quid pro quo)

Do Better
A determination to fix one's self or to tamp down guilt and shame

Have you ever thought you had to do one or more things in order to stay on God's good side? If so, what?

Are there times when you make an effort to do more so that God will be more likely to give you want you want or answer your prayers? If so, explain.

When you make a mistake or feel like you're not a "good Christian," how do you attempt to "fix" yourself or do better?

Once we begin jumping through these three religious hoops, we get stuck in a draining and discouraging cycle.

Earlier this week, I introduced the Gospel Wheel, which demonstrates God's actions and our opportunity to receive. In contrast, I've also created a Legalism Wheel. As you look at the Legalism Wheel below, take note of the outcomes associated with these actions—low confidence, comparison, criticism, and feeling "caught." This wheel illustrates the negative outcomes of the pressure to perform—whether self-induced or encouraged by others.

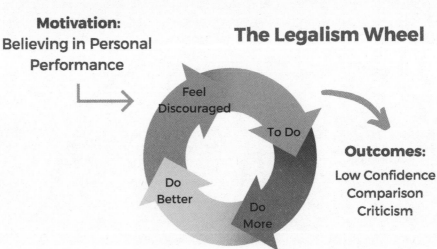

Motivation:
Believing in Personal Performance

The Legalism Wheel

Feel Discouraged

To Do

Do Better

Do More

Outcomes:
Low Confidence
Comparison
Criticism

The Judaizers in the Galatian church put pressure on the believers to ignore the gospel Paul had taught them in favor of jumping through religious hoops. While it's easy to judge them for swaying people from the gospel, we can unintentionally transfer our rules to others, too. Often, well-meaning Christians and churches create sacred cows, which are practices or processes

they fall in love with and then promote with the same zest (or more) as they do the gospel. One author writes: "Even today we find Christian groups sending the message to new believers, 'Great! Now that you believe in Christ and are saved, here's a list of things that you need to start doing to make God (and us) happy. And here's another list of things that you need to stop doing in order to be acceptable in our fellowship.'"[24]

If you've ever felt like you've been jumping through religious hoops, whether it's because you felt like you had to or because you were afraid not to, the following verse reminds us to shift our focus from others to God.

Write Galatians 1:10 in the space below:

Paul made this strong statement in response to specific allegations made against him by the Judiazers. One commentator points out that the Judaizers characterized Paul as someone who went along to get along with whomever he was with at the time. The argument of these Judaizers sounded like this: "When Paul is with the Jews, he lives like the Jews; but when he is with the Gentiles, he lives like the Gentiles. He is a man-pleaser, and therefore you cannot trust him."[25]

Did Paul go along to get along, compromising himself so that he could get an audience? Not at all! While Paul writes in 1 Corinthians 9:22 about finding common ground with everyone so that he can share the gospel with them, finding common ground isn't the same as compromise.

As I've mentioned, I worked on the staff of my local church for many years. Our founding senior pastor envisioned a place where unchurched or spiritually restless individuals could come and feel welcome, especially if they'd never been to church before. Over the years, he took lots of criticism for things such as playing secular songs with a theme that matched the sermon, serving free pop and coffee, as well as advertising heavily on radio and television before that became a regular thing for churches to do. Even though his focus remained on making connections with unchurched people and thousands of people heard the gospel message at our church each year, it was other Christians who criticized him the most.

"These Judaizers...were cowardly compromisers who mixed law and grace, hoping to please both Jews and Gentiles, but never asking whether or not they were pleasing God."[26]

What's the difference between finding common ground in order to share the gospel and compromising? (There are no wrong answers here.)

Why do you think that some Christians confuse establishing common ground with compromising?

When do you feel the people-pleasing tug in your life?

For me, the tug to people-please isn't very strong, but it's still there. In the past, I jumped through the To-Do hoop because I saw other women at church doing it and I wanted to be in their "inner circle." I thought that if I looked like them on the outside then I would be accepted. To be clear, those women weren't asking me to jump through that To-Do hoop; that was on me. Even when I've been in church events where I felt pressure to act or conform to whatever everyone else was doing, I still had the opportunity to choose whether I was acting because my focus was on God or because I was afraid of looking less Christian to others.

Can you relate? Paul teaches us that when it comes to the most important matters, such as the gospel, there's no place for people-pleasing. Our goal is to live for the God who loves us, saves us, changes us, and gives us purpose. God doesn't want you to jump through human hoops because He wants to give you so much more!

Prayer

God, help me to remember that my relationship with You is based on what You want me to receive from You, and that I don't need to follow a bunch of rules. Open my eyes to the To-Do, Do-More, and Do-Better hoops in my life. I want to trust in Your perfect promises, not find salvation in my performance; in Jesus's name. Amen.

Day 5: Spiritual Breakthrough

Big Idea

Spiritual breakthrough is an ah-ha moment when we recognize that God is at work within us, receive what He's doing, and respond to it.

At the beginning of this week's study, we read about Jesus standing in the synagogue before His hometown crowd and declaring that He had come to bring good news and to set the captives free. The audience marveled at Jesus's teaching that He came to set the captives free but then turned against Him when He implied that He would not be able to do this work in His own hometown because of their unbelief. They didn't believe that Jesus was the Messiah, nor did they believe that He had the power to free them.

Sometimes, we question whether God can really free us from the prisons in which we feel trapped. We know that if we can just break free, then we would fly and live our dreams. However, the prisons of our past, our problems, and our pain feel like walls closing in around us, keeping us from realizing our hopes and dreams.

On the cover of this study is a picture of a butterfly. Before a caterpillar becomes a butterfly, it wraps itself into a hard shell, or chrysalis. In my opinion, there's nothing attractive or interesting about a chrysalis. It looks like a prison that has trapped a caterpillar inside. Yet, it's not a prison, but rather a staging ground for transformation. Inside the caterpillar are groups of cells called imaginal discs, which are the building blocks for the new structure of the caterpillar.[27]

That little caterpillar's insides and outsides are reformed into a new body with new abilities and a new purpose. However, it's still the same creature. Those changes aren't always apparent to the naked eye, even though scientists have found a way to study them. It's not until the butterfly emerges from its shell that the final transformation can be seen.

How does a butterfly break out of its chrysalis? It pushes its wings against the wall of the chrysalis until the enclosure weakens and gives way. One of the side effects of the butterfly pushing with its wings is that they become stronger so that it is prepared to fly.

Perhaps the journey of change or metamorphosis of the butterfly can cast a vision for you, especially if you feel trapped in any prison of your past, pain, or problems—perhaps afraid that you aren't good enough for God. What if you changed your perspective from seeing yourself imprisoned to seeing those experiences as preparation?

The Gospel Wheel reminds us that it is God at work within us—loving us, saving us, changing us, and giving us purpose. Our role is to receive and

"And I am certain that God, who began the good work within you, will continue his work until it is finally finished on the day when Christ Jesus returns."

(Philippians 1:6)

"It is not by force nor by strength, but by my Spirit, says the LORD of Heaven's Armies."

(ZEchariah 4:6)

allow God to work so that we can experience the power of the gospel in our lives and the freedom that comes with it. The gospel recuses and releases us to discover God's great adventure of faith and purpose. Then we're free like that butterfly to be sent and used by God to make a difference in our world.

Yet sometimes, just like the chrysalis shields the transformation of the caterpillar into a butterfly, we don't always see where God's hand is shaping and remolding us so that we can live and love as He does. When we can't see God at work, we might question if He is working. So, how do we know that God is a work?

God Is Always at Work in Us

The apostle Paul encourages us that God is always at work, even when we can't see it.

Read Philippians 1:6 in the margin. Where is God's work taking place, and how long will God be at work?

Now read Zachariah 4:6 in the margin. How does God work in us?

God never gives up on us! As we learned earlier this week, the gospel is based on God's perfect promises, not our performance. While we might feel like that caterpillar trapped inside of a chrysalis, all messed up and disorganized on the inside, God is at work. Like the imaginal discs that God created for the caterpillar, God's power never stops working in our lives.

One of the enticements of legalism is the temptation to judge our spiritual growth or transformation according to our actions. Just because someone reads her Bible every day of the year doesn't mean that she has allowed God to reshape or transform her heart. But, what if we took the focus off of what *we* are doing and shifted to noticing where *God* is working in us?

Sometimes, we get distracted or discouraged, so we don't see where God is working in our lives. At other times, we don't see where God is working until we share our story with others. It's in our story that we see God's power working through us, not for our glory but for God's alone.

Read Galatians 1:13-24, and complete the following statements with T or F.

_____ 1. When Paul followed the Jewish religion, he did not persecute God's church. (v. 13)

_____ 2. Paul was very committed to the traditions of his religion. (v. 13)

_____ 3. Paul recognized that God had saved him by grace in spite of everything he had done. (v. 15)

_____ 4. Paul went to Arabia instead of going to Jerusalem. (v. 17)

_____ 5. Ten years later, Paul came back and visited Barnabas. (v. 18)

_____ 6. Paul stayed with Peter and also met Jesus's brother, James. (vv. 18-19)

_____ 7. Paul visited churches in Syria and Cilicia. (v. 21)

_____ 8. The church in Judea didn't know Paul personally. (v. 22)

_____ 9. Paul reports that those churches gave God glory because of him. (v. 24)

As you read through Paul's story, you can see two of the main themes that we've discussed this week. First, Paul received the gospel, and second, Paul's relationship with God through Christ wasn't about rules or seeking the approval of others.

Why did Paul give his entire story in his letter to the Galatians? There's something about hearing a person's story of life change that draws us in and helps us understand how spiritual concepts like the gospel look "with skin on" and in action.

Throughout the New Testament as Jesus meets people, we see the gospel rescue them from their sin and release them from the prison of their pain, past, or problems. Many of those people were condemned by the Pharisees for breaking the rules. Yet, Jesus moved toward them in relationship and released them from religious hoops, judgment, and shame.

In Luke 19, Jesus travels through Jericho on His way to Jerusalem. As He walks through town, Jesus seeks out a man. This encounter paints a beautiful picture of the power of the gospel as a gift we're to receive so that we can be released.

Read Luke 19:1-10 below.

¹*Jesus entered Jericho and made his way through the town.* ²*There was a man there named Zacchaeus. He was the chief tax collector in the region, and he had become very rich.* ³*He tried to get a look at Jesus, but he was too short to see over the crowd.* ⁴*So he ran ahead and climbed a sycamore-fig tree beside the road, for Jesus was going to pass that way.*

⁵*When Jesus came by, he looked up at Zacchaeus and called him by name. "Zacchaeus!" he said. "Quick, come down! I must be a guest in your home today."*

⁶*Zacchaeus quickly climbed down and took Jesus to his house in great excitement and joy.* ⁷*But the people were displeased. "He has gone to be the guest of a notorious sinner," they grumbled.*

⁸*Meanwhile, Zacchaeus stood before the Lord and said, "I will give half my wealth to the poor, Lord, and if I have cheated people on their taxes, I will give them back four times as much!"*

⁹*Jesus responded, "Salvation has come to this home today, for this man has shown himself to be a true son of Abraham.* ¹⁰*For the Son of Man came to seek and save those who are lost."*

Complete this picture by drawing and labeling the actions from the story. Or, if you prefer, summarize the story in writing in the space on the following page.

Story Summary:

Zacchaeus's name means "pure" or "righteous one,"[28] but that's not the reputation that he has. His job as a tax collector means that he works for the government oppressing the people and cheating his fellow Jews. So, when Jesus comes to town specifically looking for the man whom everyone despises, that surely draws a lot of attention.

While there isn't a moment where we see Zacchaeus come to the altar, take the pastor's hands, and pray the sinner's prayer, God was clearly at work in his life!

> **What are three ways you can see God at work in Zacchaeus's life even though it's not spelled out in the story? Look at verses 3, 6, and 8.**
>
> 1.
>
> 2.
>
> 3.

Extra Insight

"Zacchaeus was not saved because he promised to do good works. He was saved because he responded by faith to Christ's gracious word to him."[29]

Your ideas may be different than mine, but here are a few things to consider. First, Zacchaeus goes looking for Jesus. The Scriptures tell us that God loves us, and in His love He draws us to Him (Jeremiah 31:3). Then, Zacchaeus responds to Jesus's desire to visit Zacchaeus's home with great joy. Zacchaeus says "yes" to Jesus visiting his physical home, but Zacchaeus also seems to accept the invitation for Jesus to make His home in Zacchaeus's heart, too (see Ephesians 3:17 in the margin). Finally, Zacchaeus's heart is changed and he freely offers to restore others by returning what he has overcharged them—and more.

Then Christ will make his home in your hearts as you trust in him.

(Ephesians 3:17)

Many in the crowd are upset that Jesus is visiting the home of a dishonest man who breaks the religious and social rules. However, Jesus rescues Zacchaeus rather than asking him to do more or do better, and Zacchaeus receives the gift of salvation.

Zacchaeus's story is a reminder to me that we can't always see the details of what or how God is working in someone's life, but we can be assured that God is always at work. The same goes for you. Even if you don't always feel like God is at work, as long as you are praying for Him to lead you to freedom, you can be confident that He is doing exactly that!

While your journey toward freedom is a process, you can train yourself to see where God is working in you.

Spiritual Breakthrough: Identifying Where God Is Working in Your Life

The term *spiritual breakthrough* is not in the Bible, and people define it in different ways. This is the definition I am using in our study: A spiritual breakthrough is an ah-ha moment when we recognize that God is at work within us, receive what He's doing, and respond to it.

Breakthrough = Recognize + Receive + Respond

Just as a caterpillar's transformation inside a chrysalis is not readily seen with the naked eye, so we cannot always see where God is at work in our hearts, minds, and lives. Rather than using our ability to follow rules as a measuring stick for our faith, we can practice noticing where God is at work in us. Philippians 1:6 reminds us that God is always at work in us. This means that when we practice recognizing where God is transforming us, we're less likely to try to force changes in ourselves.

I have identified six kinds of ah-ha moments that capture various ways God can be at work in our lives. Beginning next week, I'll insert a reminder at the end of each day's lesson, prompting you to reflect on your study and life experience and look for any ah-ha moments when you've seen God at work. A spiritual breakthrough does not have to be a Fourth of July fireworks moment, though sometimes it can be. Most often, however, it is an observation similar to watching a caterpillar transform into a butterfly—a moment when you recognize a small way that God is transforming you from the inside out!

Prayer

God, I want to experience Your spiritual breakthrough in my life. I want to believe that Jesus came to set me free from the fears that are keeping me from experiencing the great adventure of joy and purpose that You have for my life. Help me to develop Your spiritual vision so that I can recognize where You are at work within me, receive what You're doing, and respond to Your work in my life; in Jesus's name. Amen.

Weekly Breakthrough Reflection Exercise

To close out our week of study and help you become familiar with the six kinds of ah-ha moments, spend some time reflecting on them and recording any examples *from your past* that come to mind—or examples you've observed in someone else's life. You might think of an example for only one or two of them, or you might be able to identify an example for each one. (We will be looking for *current* examples throughout the rest of our study.)

Lightbulb
You gain new understanding about God or yourself.

Describe the moment:

_____
_____
_____

Butterfly
You surrender or let go of a struggle, sin, or stronghold from your past.

Describe the moment:

_____
_____
_____

Rainbow
You find new or renewed hope based on God's promises for your life.

Describe the moment:

_____
_____
_____

Busted Brick Wall
You confront and face up to any kind of fear or worry.

Describe the moment:

_____
_____
_____

Line in the Sand
You realize that a sin, struggle, or stronghold is no longer acceptable.

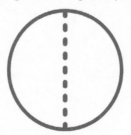

Describe the moment:

_____
_____
_____

Split-the-Rock
You have a supernatural shift in your faith or circumstances after faithfully praying and letting God lead.

Describe the moment:

_____
_____
_____

Video Viewer Guide
WEEK 1

Scriptures: Luke 4:18-19, Romans 5:16, Romans 6:23, Ephesians 2:8, Galatians 1:6-7,

Ephesians 2:9

The gospel set us free from the prisons of our _____, our _____, and

our _____.

The gospel is about _____ from God rather than following _____.

Hoops We Jump Through in Order to Earn God's Favor:

    1. _____ _____ — Attempting to gain forgiveness or save ourselves

    2. _____ _____ — Trying to please God and stack up "points"

    3. _____ _____ — Working harder after we've made a mistake

Spiritual breakthrough is an ah-ha moment when we _____ that God is at work

within us, _____ what He's doing, and _____ to it.

Freedom Principle #1

The gospel is based on God's perfect _____,

not our _____.

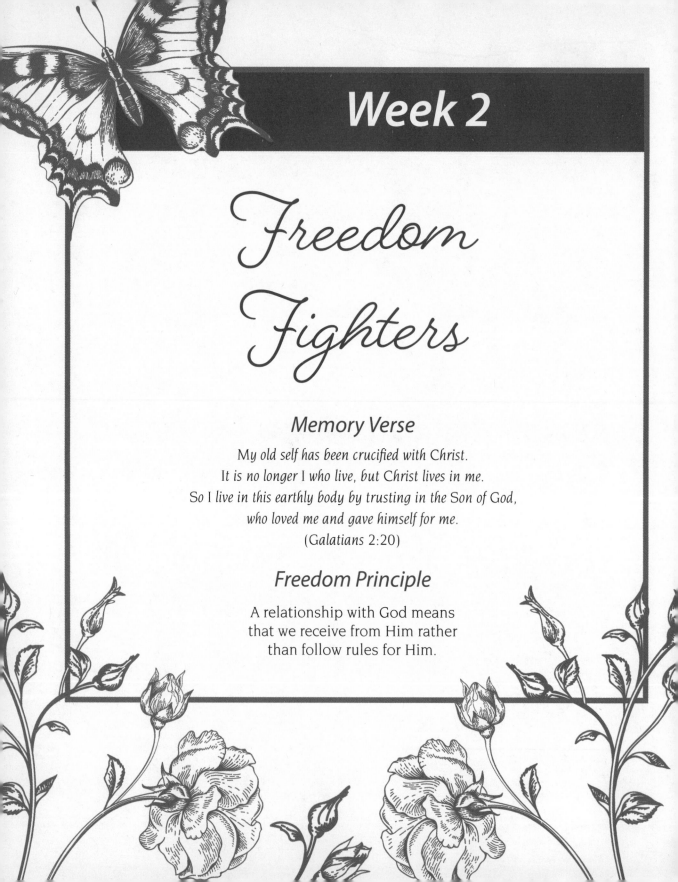

Week 2

Freedom Fighters

Memory Verse

My old self has been crucified with Christ.
It is no longer I who live, but Christ lives in me.
So I live in this earthly body by trusting in the Son of God,
who loved me and gave himself for me.
(Galatians 2:20)

Freedom Principle

A relationship with God means
that we receive from Him rather
than follow rules for Him.

At the time that I'm writing this, we're in the midst of a worldwide pandemic, and many people are not physically attending services at their churches. Some churches are meeting, and some are not. It has been an extraordinary season in our lifetimes that we'll be talking about for generations to come.

The pandemic changed our traditional relationship with church—including those churches who were already streaming services online. For many churches, the pandemic forced them to depart from long-held traditions in order to adapt. I spoke at a women's event the week before the quarantine went into effect, and the women's ministry leader proudly showed a Facebook Live recording of her church's first online service in their over 150-year history. Since then, as the pandemic has continued, I've seen people express a lot of strong and conflicting opinions regarding whether they are in favor of resuming in-person worship or continuing to participate through online worship services. And this is only one of many distractions and divisions affecting the worldwide church. Others include differing doctrinal opinions, political and social conflict, personal preferences, and interpersonal disagreements.

Yet, when we as God's people agree on the priority of the gospel, this compels us to rally together. Even now in my city and in other cities across the nation, pastors from a cross-section of churches and denominations are safely meeting to pray and plan together as they work toward addressing the challenges facing their people. The gospel has the power to bring us together in true freedom.

This week, we'll learn about a private meeting and a public confrontation, two instances that provide important lessons on why the gospel must always remain our primary focus at all times and in every season.

Day 1: Agreeing Together

While there are differing opinions on when Paul wrote Galatians, most scholars agree it was less than thirty years after Jesus's resurrection. In the scheme of things, the gospel message and the church were still relatively new. In Galatians 2, which is the focus of our study today, Paul continues his conversation about three things: 1) what happened at the Jerusalem Council (recorded in Acts 15); 2) how church leaders navigated a tough issue by agreeing together that the gospel is based on God's perfect promises, not personal performance; and 3) the idea that a relationship with God begins with receiving from God rather than following rules for God. Let's dive in!

Big Idea

Grace brings people together, but rules distract and divide.

Timeline of Paul's Life and the Early Church[1]

AD 5	Paul (Saul) born
AD 30	Crucifixion of Jesus; Pentecost
AD 35	Stephen martyred; Paul converted
AD 35-37	Paul in Damascus and Arabia
AD 38	Paul goes to Jerusalem for the first time
AD 47-49	Paul's First Missionary Journey (Antioch)[2]
AD 48	Galatians written (based on Southern Galatian theory)[3]
AD 49	Paul and Barnabas travel to Jerusalem Council
AD 50-57	Galatians written (based on Northern Galatians theory)[4]
AD 57	Paul's Letter to the Romans[5]

Read Galatians 2:1. How many years had passed since Paul's first and second trips to Jerusalem after his conversation on the road to Damascus?

Who traveled with Paul?

_____ and _____

Here in chapter 2, Paul writes a historical record of what happened when he went back to Jerusalem for the second time. If you refer to the timeline, you'll see that Paul met Christ and was converted around AD 35. On his first visit to Jerusalem, it took the people a minute to warm up to Paul (Acts 9:26-30). After all, they only knew him as the guy who had killed Christians. In order to change their minds, someone with tremendous influence had to speak up for Paul.

Read Acts 9:27 in the margin. Who spoke up on behalf of Paul, and what did he say?

But Barnabas took him and brought him to the apostles. He told them how Saul on his journey had seen the Lord and that the Lord had spoken to him, and how in Damascus he had preached fearlessly in the name of Jesus.

(Acts 9:27 NIV)

Read Acts 4:36–37 in the margin. What do these verses tell you about the kind of man Barnabas was?

36 Joseph, a Levite from Cyprus, who the apostles called Barnabas (which means "son of encouragement"), 37 sold a field he owned and brought the money and put it at the apostles' feet.

(Acts 4:36–37 NIV)

Don't we wish every Christian that we met had the heart of Barnabas? Since my given name includes most of the letters in his name, I aspire to be just like him! With his track record of encouragement, generosity, and faith, it's no surprise that Barnabas had the kind of influence necessary to speak to the apostles on Paul's behalf. (We'll get to Titus in a bit.)

Thanks to Barnabas, Paul was accepted by the apostles after his conversion. He preached the gospel in Jerusalem until some Greek-speaking Jews tried to kill him (Acts 9:29). The new Christian believers took charge of getting him out of town.

Read Galatians 2:2. Why did Paul say that he went back to Jerusalem this time?

What kind of meeting did Paul have with the Jerusalem church leaders?

What was Paul's main goal in meeting with the leaders of the church?

Paul's trip to Jerusalem appears to be motivated by a revelation from God. The first time he was in Jerusalem, some Jews had tried to kill him. This time, Paul met privately with the church leaders to make sure that they were all on the same page when it came to the gospel message. His concern was that if he taught one version of the gospel and the Jerusalem leaders preached a different way of salvation, then the influence and effectiveness of the gospel would collapse.

Read Galatians 2:3 (NLT). What was the outcome of Paul's meeting with the other apostles?

What did they *not* demand of Titus?

Why was this signficant?

The fact that the Jerusalem apostles did not demand that Titus be circumcised was a big deal. As one source notes, "The Jerusalem apostles agreed that it is faith in Christ alone, and not any other performance or ritual, that is necessary for salvation. Their acceptance of Titus was proof that they had accepted Paul's ministry and these radical implications of the gospel."[7]

Extra Insights

"Paul first mentions Titus in Galatians 2:1-3. As an uncircumcised Gentile, Titus accompanied Paul and Barnabas to Jerusalem as a living example of a great theological truth: Gentiles need not be circumcised in order to be saved."[6]

In Galatians 2:9, Paul talks about the pillars of the church, James, Peter and John. Peter preached after the Day of Pentecost with tremendous results that fueled the early church (Acts 2). John, one of Jesus's closest disciples, referred to himself as "the disciple whom Jesus loved" (John 21:20 NIV). James, Jesus's brother (Matthew 13:55), became a believer when Jesus appeared to him after the Resurrection (1 Corinthians 15:5-7) and later became the leader of the church in Jerusalem.

As we learned last week, Judaizers and other false teachers were demanding that circumcision be added to the gospel. Believing that salvation by faith alone was too much like "easy believism,"[8] they rejected the notion of the free gift of salvation. As part of the terms and conditions of God's covenant to protect and provide for the them, circumcision was the Israelites' "signature" of agreement. However, circumcision was always intended to be a ritual symbol in the Israelites' covenant, not a saving act.

Covenants are serious business! A biblical covenant is a specific agreement between God and His people, and that agreement includes specific promises that He makes to them.[9] In the coming weeks of our study, we'll explore three coventants: the Abrahamic covenant, the Mosaic covenant, and the new covenant. These covenants are important to know and understand because they demonstrate how serious God is about loving us and wanting an exclusive relationship with us.

Read Ephesians 2:11-18, and fill in the blanks below (NIV).

1. Gentiles were un_____. (v. 11)

2. C_____ was completed by human hands. (v. 11)

3. Gentiles who were once far away are now brought n_____ by the blood of Christ. (v. 13)

4. Christ is our p_____ because he set aside the l_____. (vv. 14-15)

5. His purpose was to create in himself one h_____ out of two. (v. 15)

6. For through him, both Jews and Gentiles have access to the F_____. (v. 18)

In Ephesians 2, Paul explains how Jesus came to remove the need for the people to jump through the religious hoops that the law required. However, believers then and now still have trouble putting down those hoops, because some of us hope that the more rituals, traditions, and rules we follow, the less we will fear falling short of earning God's approval. But that isn't the gospel at all! As one source explains, "Grace means salvation completely apart from any merit or works on our part. We can add nothing to it; we dare take nothing from it."[10]

Scholars debate whether the meeting referenced in Galatians 2 was the Jerusalem Council meeting or another meeting in advance of that.[11] In any case, while Paul came to meet privately, some false teachers showed up to spy on what was happening and stir things up.

Again, the timeline of this meeting might be debated,[12] but not the details of what Paul writes about in chapter 2. Paul gets to the heart of the matter regarding why God revealed to him the need to travel there. While the apostles in Jerusalem were called to preach the gospel to the Jews and Paul was called to preach to the Gentiles, Paul wanted to make sure that everyone was preaching the same message.

We have a similar struggle today, don't we? We have one gospel, yet we have so many different churches, denominations, and opinions. It's a great tension that has caused all kinds of heartache for centuries. Let's consider some lessons in unity that we can derive from Paul's writing in Galatians 2, especially when important matters of faith come up.

1. When it comes to church matters, there's a difference between secret and private.

Notice how verse 2 says that Paul met privately with the church leaders. *Private* does not mean that Paul was trying to hide his presence or his agenda. Rather, he chose to meet directly with those who were in leadership without the case-making or consensus-building that might happen with crowds around him. Secrecy, on the other hand, happens when those in influence try to hide what's happening because they don't want details to come to light. Paul's aim was the exact opposite of that. He wanted to make sure that unity, not secrecy, was the outcome.

Is there a conflict in your church right now that has worsened because of case-making or consensus-building? If so, do you need to extract yourself from the secret conversations, gossip, or pot-stirring? Write your thoughts below:

What would be more helpful and God-honoring instead?

You may not be able to stop others from gossiping or speculating about church matters, but you don't have to be a part of it. If you feel the need to talk about what's going on, perhaps it's best to talk to God in prayer.

2. We need others we can lean on for support and accountability.

Paul took Barnabas and Titus with him to Jerusalem. Barnabas was an encourager, so he would have been a blessing to Paul on the trip, especially when facing the difficulties from false teachers that they encountered. Paul loved Jesus, but he wasn't perfect. Although there's nothing in the text to suggest that Paul struggled with attitude issues, I imagine that Barnabas and Titus were good friends to have around for encouragement and accountability, especially during those difficult discussions.

It's always good for us to have trusted friends who share our faith, especially when challenges come up and we need support. You want to have one or two friends who can encourage you and point you toward the gospel in those times.

Who are two friends who encourage you and point you toward living the gospel?

Trusted voices and faithful friends know us and our struggles with the To-Do, Do-More, and Do-Better hoops. Pray for God to give your friends wisdom to speak into your life. And if you're waiting for God to send Christian friends, keep praying and don't give up!

3. When conflict arises, we can remain unified on the gospel.

There are a lot of hot-button issues in the church today. Depending on your background or denomination, you might be dealing with a few of those issues now. There's a difference between being discerning about secondary issues and defending the gospel. Don't let differences on secondary issues distract you from the gospel message!

If there ever was a hill to die on, this is it: the centrality of the gospel. Just as Paul and the leaders in Jerusalem refused to give in, even for a single moment, we too must stand strong on the gospel. Nowhere do we read that Paul and the other leaders were mean, disrespectful, violent, or disparaging toward the false teachers—only that they preserved the truth of the gospel.

Is there any secondary issue at your church distracting you these days? If so, what is it?

What are some clues or indicators that you're overly distracted?

What would it look like for you to live out the gospel even though there may be distractions around you? (*Clue*: Reflect on the Gospel Wheel on page 22.)

This one can be hard! Depending on your experience, you may have witnessed some tough moments in your community of faith over various issues. Yet, you can choose to stand for the gospel no matter what is happening around you. Stand strong and don't let other issues distract you from putting your time, your heart, and your passion into sharing the gospel with those who need it.

Today we've seen that the stakes of Paul's visit to Jerusalem were high. Again, there are some striking parallels between what Paul and the church leaders faced and what we are encountering in our world today. Be encouraged! Just as they unified under the gospel in the face of pressure, we can do the same. The same power that raised Jesus from the dead empowers us to stand up against those who want to tear down and divide the church. If your church community is or has been facing difficult issues, my heart goes out to you. Yet even in the midst of conflict, you can decide to champion the gospel and trust God to work everything else out.

Prayer

Dear God, You love the church more than I do. Help me to recognize the difference between defending the gospel and becoming distracted by lesser matters. Open my eyes to see where I need to keep the main thing the main thing and not participate in potentially divisive debates or situations that can create disunity. I want to have boldness like Paul, be an encourager like Barnabas, and demonstrate faith like Titus; in Jesus's name. Amen.

Ah-ha Moment

Did you notice any ah-ha spiritual breakthrough moments in today's study, your prayer time, or your daily activities? If so, record that moment on the final page of this week's study (page 73).

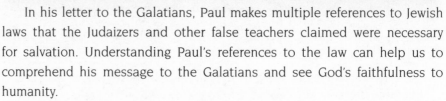

Day 2: Breaking Through Traditions of the Past

Big Idea

Jesus fulfilled the law for our freedom.

In his letter to the Galatians, Paul makes multiple references to Jewish laws that the Judaizers and other false teachers claimed were necessary for salvation. Understanding Paul's references to the law can help us to comprehend his message to the Galatians and see God's faithfulness to humanity.

In the Old Testament, we learn that God gave the law to the Israelites after He freed them from over four hundred years of slavery in Egypt. God didn't give the law because He wanted the Israelites to jump through a lot of complicated hoops. Rather, the law was part of a covenant agreement that He had made to Abraham centuries earlier (see Genesis 12 and 17; we will study this in Week 3).

Paul's references to the law likely refer to the Torah or the first five books of the Old Testament. (The term *Torah* also is used to refer to the entire Hebrew Bible, which includes divinely inspired books of wisdom and writings from the prophets.) The role of the Torah was defined as "the way to live based upon the Covenant that God made with His people."[13] So, the Torah provided teaching for God's people as to how to live in a relationship with Him.

Many scholars agree that Moses wrote the Torah, also known as the *Pentateuch*, though other scholars suggest that there may have been other writers.[14] Regardless, ancient and contemporary Jews alike consider the Torah the main authority for living out their covenant relationship with God.[15]

Within the Torah, Moses recorded God's biblical law, which was a code of conduct "established by direct revelation from God to direct His people in their worship, in their relationship to Him, and in their social relationships with each other." Later, this code of conduct was expanded by rabbis who incorporated 613 precepts or rules into the Torah after the Jewish people returned from captivity in Babylon.[16]

One of the most well-known portions of biblical law is the Ten Commandments recorded in Exodus 20. Moses recorded these on Mount Sinai, and while the Ten Commandments weren't intended to be a means of salvation, these commandments provide instruction in moral living that still applies today.

In light of the gospel, we no longer rely upon the law for our relationship with God. As we've seen in John 3:16, John 14:6, and other verses we've studied together, we are saved through Jesus's sacrifice for us. However, our human tendency is to believe that we can save ourselves if we follow the right rules. So, Paul refers to the law often because many in his audience seem to believe that their salvation comes from following the Torah's rules, and he compels them to believe that the gospel of grace is enough.

While the law instructed the Israelites in how they should live in a way that reflected God's character, the covenants or agreements that God established through Abraham, Moses, and the new covenant demonstrated not only His character but also His love and plan for His people.

The covenants that God entered into with Abraham and Moses were eventually replaced with a new covenant based on Jesus Christ. Next week, we'll study the relationship between those three covenants. For now, let's consider why faith in Jesus, rather than wearing ourselves out trying to follow religious rules, leads us to freedom. Today we'll learn about the new covenant that supports the gospel Paul preaches to the Galatian church. Understanding the new covenant and how it applies to us is vital to confidently trusting that God is at work within us, leading us toward freedom in Christ.

Read Hebrews 8:6-10, and answer the following questions with T (true) or F (false).

_____ 1. The new covenant will be better than the old one. (v. 6)

_____ 2. The second covenant was needed to replace the first covenant. (v. 7)

_____ 3. The Israelites remained faithful to God's covenant. (v. 9)

_____ 4. God would write His law on their hearts. (v. 10)

This passage from Hebrews references what God spoke through the prophet Jeremiah in the Old Testament (Jeremiah 31). The covenant that God created was perfect, but the Israelites were not (Hebrews 8:8-9). In the midst of what seems like a lot of daunting rules, the old covenant revealed God's love, mercy, and protection for His people, even as they fell short. While the people could memorize the do's and don'ts of the law, that same law was unable to give them the internal power they needed. Knowledge did not mean power. Yet, as Hebrews 8:6 points out, God had better promises in mind when sending Christ. As one source states, "Christ himself is the New Testament covenant—a covenant that cannot fail and cannot be broken."[19]

Extra Insights

"God's law, unlike those of the other nations of the ancient world, viewed all human life as especially valuable, because people are created in God's image. Thus, biblical law was more humane."[17]

"When you became a Christian, you received a new heart and mind. You were born again....You received a new spiritual radar—a new ability to perceive spiritual things. You now have the capacity to experience God and obey him. But while every Christian has this ability, not every Christian has developed it."[18]

In the same way, he took the cup of wine after supper, saying, "This cup is the new covenant between God and his people—an agreement confirmed with my blood. Do this in remembrance of me as often as you drink it."

1 Corinthians 11:25

Lay your hand on the animal's head, and the LORD will accept its death in your place to purify you, making you right with him.

(Leviticus 1:4)

On the night before He was crucified, Jesus spoke to His disciples and told them about a new covenant and how it would be guaranteed.

Read 1 Corinthians 11:25 in the margin. What did Jesus say would confirm God's new covenant with His people?

Jesus would give His lifeblood to guarantee our salvation and make it possible for us to gain right standing with God. As Jesus shared this with His disciples, they would have known that the previous covenants required the sacrifice of blood, namely the blood of animals sacrificed to make atonement or penance for sin (Leviticus 17:11).

In our modern times, talking about animal sacrifices may seem savage, but in ancient cultures, people hunted animals not only for food but also for many other uses, including religious sacrifice. For the Israelites, the act of killing an animal was a symbolic reminder that sin is serious business.

Read Leviticus 1:4 in the margin. In order for God to accept the animal sacrifice as atonement for sin, what did a person have to do before the animal was killed?

Why do you think that God required this?

That's pretty sobering, isn't it? A person had to rest his or her hand on the animal's head before it was killed as atonement for their sins. God wanted His people to personally identify with the consequence of sin, which is death—whether spiritual death or the death of trust, relationships, or one's well-being (Romans 6:23). However, the new covenant in Christ ended the need for atonement through animal sacrifice.

Read Hebrews 9:13-14. What is the difference between animal sacrifices and Jesus's sacrifice?

Personally, I feel really great about no more animal sacrifices! On a serious note, the reason we no longer need animal sacrifices is because Jesus was the final and full sacrifice for our sins. One source explains that the new covenant "refers to the new relationship that God establishes through the death, burial, and resurrection of Jesus Christ. If you are a Christian, one who has trusted in Jesus as the substitutionary atoning sacrifice for your sins, you are a member of the new covenant—along with the rest of the people of God."[20]

At the beginning of today's lesson, we considered the law that accompanied the covenants. We might wonder if the law was a mistake since God sent Jesus to be the new covenant for us. Not at all!

Read Matthew 5:17 in the margin. What do you think Jesus meant by saying that He came to accomplish or fulfill the law?

One scholar says that Jesus "had come to honor the law and help God's people love it, learn it, and live it."[21] Therefore, Jesus didn't come to get rid of the law. After all, the law reflects God's perfect and sovereign character. Jesus came to fulfill or satisfy the requirements of the law that God's people could not do on their own.

In today's lesson there may be new information you're absorbing. You can always refer back to this lesson as we continue our study. As we will see throughout Paul's letter to the Galatians, he refers repeatedly to some of the Galatians' legalistic usage of the law to try to earn their salvation or favor with God. By now, I pray that you're beginning to see that their point of view is wrong.

As you reflect on your life, are there To-Do, Do-More, or Do-Better hoops that you still jump through out of habit, fear of letting someone down, or extra insurance with God "just in case"? If so, what are they?

"Don't misunderstand why I have come. I did not come to abolish the law of Moses or the writings of the prophets. No, I came to accomplish their purpose."
(Matthew 5:17)

Read Colossians 2:20-23 below. Paul's words are direct and powerful. Underline the portions that resonate with you. Write any thoughts or observations in the margin.

²⁰You have died with Christ, and he has set you free from the spiritual powers of this world. So why do you keep on following the rules of the world, such as, ²¹"Don't handle! Don't taste! Don't touch!"? ²²Such rules are mere human teachings about things that deteriorate as we use them. ²³These rules may seem wise because they require strong devotion, pious self-denial, and severe bodily discipline. But they provide no help in conquering a person's evil desires.

Though our culture and customs are different than those of the Jewish and Gentile believers of Paul's day, we still struggle with thinking that we need to follow rules in order to please God. My prayer is that today's lesson gives you an even greater appreciation of the gift of the gospel in your life. Jesus came to fulfill the law and establish Himself as the new covenant, not so that you could be spared from following rules and jumping through hoops, but so that you could experience true freedom in Him—freedom that brings spiritual breakthrough and heart transformation. And that's a gift that could never come from following a bunch of rules.

Prayer

God, I am so grateful that You had better promises in mind than the old covenant. Thank You for sending Christ to die for my sin. Thank You for the freedom that the gospel brings into my life. I want to live in Your freedom; in Jesus's name. Amen.

Day 3: The Poison of Hypocrisy

Hypocrisy is a hot button topic because many of us have experienced deep hurt or heartache when someone who says they are a Christian has done or said things Christians shouldn't do or say. In his book *Answers to Tough Questions Skeptics Ask About the Christian Faith*, author Josh McDowell observes that one of the major reasons people reject the gospel of grace is because they've seen Christians behave in horrible, immoral, or criminal ways. He writes,

Christianity does not stand or fall on the way Christians have acted throughout history or are acting today. Christianity stands or falls on the person of Jesus, and Jesus was not a hypocrite. . . . Since Christianity depends on Jesus, it is incorrect to try to invalidate the Christian faith by pointing out horrible things done in the name of Christianity.[22]

As Christians, it's easy for us to point our fingers at each other when we make mistakes. Some Christians walk away from church or their faith because of another Christian's behavior.

I remember feeling hurt and betrayed by a group of people I served with many years ago. After a series of events, I felt like I didn't matter. I thought, *Christians shouldn't treat each other that way!* The rejection cut deep, and for a time, I considered leaving the church that I attended because of how I felt. Yet, I thank God that I endured that painful season. The hurt didn't magically go away, but I allowed God to work in my heart so that I didn't get stuck in that hurt; and I eventually moved on to a new area of ministry that led to where I am today. It wasn't easy, but it was worth it.

By definition, hypocrisy is the result of when our behavior doesn't match our stated beliefs. No one likes to be called a hypocrite, but we all make mistakes. We lie, even though we believe that lying is wrong. We are unloving, even though God calls us to love. We're human and, at times, we can be hypocrites. But that's not the whole story. As Josh McDowell also said, "Just because a person is not perfect does not mean that he is a phony."[23]

One of my favorite sayings is "keep your eyes on your own Hula-Hoop." As humans, we all have personal blindspots or the inability to see how our beliefs or behaviors hurt us or others. Let's be honest, it's much easier for us to see what other people are doing wrong or how they've wronged us than it is for us to see our own wrongs. However, Jesus challenges us, especially when we're judgmental toward other Christians, to examine our lives and ask God to reveal our blindspots related to our patterns of beliefs and behaviors that do not align with the gospel of grace.

> *"And why worry about a speck in your friend's eye when you have a log in your own? . . . Hypocrite! First, get rid of the log in your own eye; then you will see well enough to deal with the speck in your friend's eye."*
>
> (Matthew 7:3, 5)

In Galatians 2, Paul publicly blasts Peter for hypocritical behavior that was influencing others, leading them away from the power of the gospel of grace. It's an uncomfortable experience for Peter, but let us pay attention to his humility and consider what we can learn from his example.

Extra Insight

"A hypocrite is someone who not only does not practice what one preaches, but a person who doe the opposite of what one preaches."[24]

Read Galatians 2:11. What did Paul do when Peter came to Antioch?

Paul opposed Peter, pointing out that Peter was wrong. Before we look at what happened, it's important to note *how* Paul confronted Peter. Several translations record that Paul opposed Peter "to his face" (NLT, NIV, NASB). That sounds harsh, doesn't it? The Greek word for "oppose" is *anthistémi*, which means to "take a complete stand against" or "to forcefully declare one's personal conviction."[25] In essence, this is what Paul did. He stood up against Peter's hypocritical behavior, not to tear Peter down but to use the confrontation as a teachable moment. This verse provides a very important lesson that we need to remember in order to maintain unity with other believers. There's a difference between a confrontation that connects to a teachable moment and a confrontation that involves condemnation with threats.

Extra Insights

"Table fellowship was more than just inviting someone over for a meal; it was often considered to be a sign of acceptance and approval."[26]

Jews didn't eat with Gentiles for religious and racial reasons.[27]

"Peter's freedom was threatened by Peter's fear."[28]

Read Galatians 2:12. What, specifically, did Paul confront Peter about?

When and why did Peter change his behavior?

Now read Galatians 2:13-14.

How did Peter's hypocrisy influence others?

What question did Paul ask Peter?

The Scripture doesn't reveal exactly when Paul confronted Peter. What we can see is that Paul was around long enough to see that Barnabas and others were caught up in the side effects of Peter's legalism and hypocrisy (v. 13).

Picture Peter sitting in the "lunchroom" with the Gentiles laughing, talking, and having a good time while eating. Then, the next day, Peter shows up for lunch. However, as he's headed to sit with his Gentile friends, he sees the false teachers sitting at a table staring at them. Peter pretends he doesn't see his Gentile lunch buddies and, instead, turns his back on them.

Remember, Peter had great influence. So, the entire lunchroom would have been impacted by his actions. Jewish believers who also had started eating pork perhaps would have felt conflicted and questioned their new faith. The Gentiles would have felt rejected by Peter and also might have questioned the gospel they had heard and whether or not they were saved by grace. Imagine Barnabas. He had sacrificed so much because he believed the gospel.

This is why Paul called Peter out in front of the others. One author observes, "The public harm to the gospel had to be put right publicly."[29] But Paul didn't threaten Peter. He created a teachable moment, not a threat. Peter had preached the gospel of grace and watched as thousands said yes to the gospel in one day (Acts 2), and now he bore the pain of seeing his actions lead others away from the gospel.

Legalism and hypocrisy are like dynamite and a match. Put them together and they'll blow things apart. Since Peter blew things up publicly with his hypocrisy, accountability needed to be public too, especially since those affected needed to hear the truth as well.

God created a similar a teachable moment in Peter's life using a Roman soldier named Cornelius. He was a God-fearing man who had a vision one day. An angel of God told Cornelius to send some men to Joppa, about thirty miles away, to find Peter and bring him to Cornelius's house. Cornelius sent two servants and a soldier to bring Peter back (Acts 10:1-7).

The next day as the messengers neared Joppa, a hungry Peter went up on the roof to pray while lunch was being prepared. Being hungry, he was likely thinking about food as he fell into a trance (vv. 9-10).

Read Acts 10:11-16 and answer the following questions.

What did the voice tell Peter to do with the four-footed animals in the vision? (vv. 11-13)

What was Peter's objection? (v. 14)

What was God's reply? (v. 15)

Acts 10 also records Peter's visit to Cornelius's home. While Peter's hypocrisy might have led Barnabas and others astray, he repented. The results were stunning! When Peter arrived at Cornelius's home, it was full of guests. Peter preached the gospel and only the gospel, as we read in Acts 10:34-43. The result is recorded in verses 44-45 (NIV): "While Peter was still speaking these words, the Holy Spirit came on all who heard the message. The circumcised believers who had come with Peter were astonished that the gift of the Holy Spirit had been poured out even on Gentiles."

The power of the gospel prompted Paul to speak up and Peter to repent, creating a beautiful example for us to remember today!

It's easy to call out hypocrisy in others. But let's make it personal by following Jesus's teaching to examine ourselves before pointing out the faults of others (Matthew 7:3). There are people—family, friends, children, spouses, co-workers—watching our lives. They may see our Jesus bumper stickers on our cars or our posts about our faith on social media, but do they see the gospel lived out loud in our lives? As the well-known maxim goes, people learn more by what's caught than what's taught.

Consider this teachable moment in Peter's life, and make it personal for your own. Are there any people you aren't "eating with"? If so, explain.

Just as Peter's fear stole his freedom, what kind of fears or worries are keeping you from living God's best for you? (It's okay to be honest. You can write your answers on another piece of paper or in a journal if that feels safer.)

Reject any voice in your head, in your heart, or around you that is condemning or criticizing you. That is not God's voice. None of us is perfect. We all make mistakes. However, the beauty of the gospel is that we can always lean into God's grace at any time. Just as you didn't have to clean yourself up before knowing God, so you don't have to clean yourself up before confessing to God that you've lived differently than your words have proclaimed. God's grace is unconditional and unending.

As you wrap up today's lesson, here's an all-in-one reflection exercise and prayer to integrate what you've learned with what's happening in your heart right now.

Reflection Exercise / Prayer

1. What are some of your takeaways from today's lesson about Paul's actions and Peter's response?

2. Pray the prayer below, asking God to reveal any sin within:

Search me, God, and know my heart;
test me and know my anxious thoughts.
See if there is any offensive way in me,
and lead me in the way everlasting.
(Psalm 139:23-24 NIV)

3. What's happening in your heart right now?

4. Is there a mismatch between how you are living and what you believe? Explain.

5. Is there anything you sense God calling you to do differently? Explain.

Ah-ha Moment

Did you notice any ah-ha spiritual breakthrough moments in today's study, your prayer time, or your daily activities? If so, record that moment on the final page of this week's study (page 73).

Day 4: Just Jesus

During the fourteen years that I served on staff at my local church, I loved meeting people who showed up because there was something missing, stuck, or broken in their lives. While they entered the front doors of our church

Big Idea

In Christ alone our hope is found.

with that look on their face that often conveyed, "I didn't know what else to do," I knew that the gospel of grace could rescue them from their prison of problems, their past, or their pain.

Over the years, I connected with thousands of people who were far from God, but the gospel of grace brought them into a relationship with Him. I remember meeting one person whose family prayed hard for him for almost twenty years. He came to my new believer's class. I'd heard about his past with substance abuse, legal issues, and lots of bad decisions. However, his radiant face shone with the light that could come only from the saving power of the gospel. As our class discussed the gospel of grace, I could see his awe of Jesus's sacrifice for him. He knew that he couldn't save himself, so his "yes" to the gospel of grace wasn't tainted by the lure of religious rules. He never went to church growing up, so he didn't even know the rules! As he shared with the class, his excitement over God's forgiveness was contagious. I remember asking myself if I still had that kind of joy and excitement over the gospel of grace in my own life.

When was the last time you felt the radiance of freedom shining through you from the inside out? Today, we're going to finish our exploration of Paul's teachable moment with Peter in Galatians 2 and consider the life-giving, transforming power of justification.

Read Galatians 2:15-16 (NIV) below and follow these prompts:

Circle the word *justified* each time it appears.

Draw a cross over each occurrence of the word *faith*.

Underline the first part of verse 16.

Draw a line through *works of the law* each time it appears.

¹⁵ *"We who are Jews by birth and not sinful Gentiles* ¹⁶ *know that a person is not justified by the works of the law, but by faith in Jesus Christ. So we, too, have put our faith in Christ Jesus that we may be justified by faith in Christ and not by the works of the law, because by the works of the law no one will be justified."*

One scholar considers this section of Scripture the most important text in Paul's letter to the Galatians.³⁰ Remember, Paul addressed Peter in front of the crowd, continuing his teaching moment. First, Paul reminded Peter that they were both raised in the Jewish faith, which meant they grew up under the law or Mosaic covenant, which we studied on Day 2, and were entitled to special blessings as God's chosen people.

Then, a great "but" happens in verse 16.

Circle the word *but* in verse 16 on the previous page. Then rewrite verse 16 in your own words below:

Paul acknowledges that the law can't make Jews right with God. The law pushes the legalism wheel around with its relentless To-Do, Do-More, and Do-Better hoops. Holiness through law-keeping requires perfection, but our human effort, even our best effort, can never perfectly fulfill God's law.

The word *justified* appears three times in verses 15-16. Other translations use the phrase "right with God." *Justify* is a legal term that "refers to God's verdict of not guilty on the day of judgment."[31] The term appears in both Galatians and Romans, both written by Paul.

Justification, or righteousness, is central to the gospel of grace. A simplified explanation of justification is "just as if I never sinned"; but I want us to explore it further because it is at the root of our faith and necessary for us to understand if we are to avoid or push back against toxic rules and false teaching.

First, justification doesn't pretend that sin doesn't exist. Justification acknowledges our sin, but it also acknowledges that the price has been paid for it. One biblical scholar offers a helpful breakdown of justification using the letters ABCD:

Act   "Justification is an ***act*** of God. . . . It is . . . a legal declaration in which God pardons the sinner of all his [or her] sins and accepts and accounts the sinner as righteous in His sight."

Basis   "God justifies the sinner solely on the ***basis*** of the obedience and death of His Son, our representative, Jesus Christ."

Confess   "Sinners are justified through faith alone when they ***confess*** their trust in Christ."

8 Yes, everything else is worthless when compared with the infinite value of knowing Christ Jesus my Lord. For his sake I have discarded everything else, counting it all as garbage, so that I could gain Christ. (Philippians 3:8)

Demonstrate — "Finally, saving faith must ***demonstrate*** itself to be the genuine article by producing good works."[32]

In order to be justified, we have to recognize our need for God's rescue. One of the criticisms I hear from non-Christians is that many Christians seem to think that they are better than everyone else. Justification reminds us that we owed God a debt of sin that we couldn't pay. "We have publicly declared...that we are desperately in need of Another to give us his righteousness, to complete us, to live in us."[33]

As Paul shared in his conversion story in Galatians 1, he knew the power of justification in his own life. Therefore, Paul wasn't teaching anything that he didn't believe himself. In fact, in Philippians 3:5-6, Paul shares his spiritual résumé, which was quite impressive because he followed and excelled beyond all of the rules for being a good Jew. Yet, Paul didn't believe the hype about his old religious way of life.

Read Philippians 3:8 in the margin. How does Paul refer to all of the good, religious things that he'd done?

Extra Insight

"A life of grace walks in the reality that Jesus died to forgive the red in our ledgers, to cancel the debt of sin and offer freedom and reconciliation not by our own merit."[34]

Read Galatians 2:17-19. Are we sinners if we stop following the rules in order to follow Christ? (v. 17)

Imagine yourself in the crowd of the Galatian believers. You've been raised in a Jewish home, which means that your family observes all of the religious traditions like Passover, as well as many festivals. Since following the law concerns all aspects of your social and family life, every dinner conversation includes lectures and warnings to do better because God's blessing depends on it. Every moment of every day in your life looks like running on the legalism wheel like a hamster, trying to keep up with all of the To-Do, Do-More, and Do-Better requirements. But as one source explains, "The reason righteousness does not come by observing the law is because of human sin."[35] In other words, we will never be able to do it all perfectly.

Yet the gospel of grace means that in Christ we are freed from a life riddled with relentless to-dos to a life justified by "it's already done."

When Paul preached to the Galatians years before, they said yes to the gospel of grace, which no doubt sounded great to them. But perhaps insecurity surfaced over time. Chances are that more than one person wondered, "What if Paul was wrong? What if God wants us to keep living according to the law *and* believe in Jesus?"

> **Look again at Galatians 2:18. What do you think Paul meant when he said, "I am a sinner if I rebuild the old system of law I already tore down"?**

> **What realization did Paul come to in verse 19?**

Last week we read Paul's testimony of his life before Christ. Paul zealously dedicated his life to his religion. However, one scholar notes, "Paul never really lived for God. He was being very moral and good—but it was all for Paul, never for God."[36] That's a sobering statement, isn't it? It is possible for us to spend our entire lives never missing church, giving generously, and volunteering, yet do it all for ourselves and not for God.

What does justification look like in real life? Let's look at a story of Jesus and an immoral woman that paints a beautiful picture of what freedom through justification means.

> **Read Luke 7:36-50.**

> **How is the woman described? (v. 37)**

> **What did she do once she saw Jesus? (v. 38)**

> **How did Simon judge both the woman and Jesus? (v. 39)**

> **Summarize the story that Jesus told Simon, the Pharisee. (vv. 41-42)**

Big Idea

You've been made new!

Write Jesus's words to the woman below. (v. 50)

It's with Jesus's final words to the woman, "go in peace," that we will conclude our study today. Justification isn't a fancy term that we talk about in order to appear more spiritual. Justification is the cornerstone of the gospel that changes everything for you and me every day of our lives. If you've been a Christian for a while, I pray that today's lesson on justification has refreshed your awareness of the tremendous gift God has given to you in Christ. If you're a newer believer, I pray that today's study keeps your line of sight clear and focused on Jesus alone. He has done the work for us so that, by faith, we can believe and have peace.

What's one takeaway from today's lesson that you want to write down so that you won't forget it?

Prayer

God, what You've done for me is beyond incredible. Thank You for canceling my debt so that I can live freely for You; in Jesus's name. Amen.

Day 5: The Best Status Change Ever!

When I hear the word *status*, I think of Facebook. Ahhh, the Facebook status update. I'm not referring to writing a new post on your timeline but to announcing an update in your job, education, or relationship status. Depending on what the update is, changing your relationship status can be a dreaded or highly anticipated event (or you might not care about such things at all!).

A friend of mine survived a difficult divorce over twenty years ago. She often expressed sadness over her lack of success in dating and wondered if God had a special someone for her. One day I stopped by her office, and she smiled as she told me she had just started seeing a special someone. A few months later, I saw her relationship status on Facebook change from

"single" to "in a relationship." Another few months passed, and I was the one smiling when I noticed that her status changed again from "in a relationship" to "engaged."

In the last few verses of Galatians 2, Paul writes about the consequences of the gospel of grace: *Christ living within us*!

Now, I've been a Christ-follower for the majority of my life, and I still struggle to comprehend that the life of Christ—the reason for the gospel of grace—makes His home inside my heart. Jesus knows that my heart-home gets messy and cluttered. He knows there's some baggage from the past that needs to be cleared out. But since He's at home in my heart, I am confident of this: I never need to fear being enough for Christ because Christ lives in me.

Today's study is about the best status change of all: letting go of our old life and beginning a new life in Christ. That's the most important status update we'll ever have from now through eternity. This status change includes a new standing that promises hope and freedom. It's a status update we should get excited about!

> **Read or recall Galatians 2:20, this week's memory verse, and fill in the blanks of the first half of the verse below.**
>
> *My _____ _____ has been crucified with Christ. It is no longer I who live, but Christ _____ _____ _____.*
>
> **(Galatians 2:20a)**

When Paul writes that our old life has been crucified with Christ, he means exactly that. Picture Jesus hanging on the cross with your sins, failures, shortcomings, and struggles nailed to the cross. He died and took all of that with Him. Not only that, but when we realize that Christ lives in us, we're assured that the power of the gospel of grace, which rescues us, continues to work in our lives each day whether we've been saved for five minutes or fifty years.

> **Describe your old self before you placed your faith in Jesus Christ.**

"Christ will do everything for you, or nothing."
—Tim Keller[37]

At what point did you realize that you need Christ in your life? Describe what happened.

Describe a moment in the past or present when you've seen Christ at work in your life and knew the gospel of grace was alive in you.

[7] *But in fact, it is best for you that I go away, because if I don't, the Advocate won't come. If I do go away, then I will send him to you.* [8] *And when he comes, he will convict the world of its sin, and of God's righteousness, and of the coming judgment."*

(John 16:7-8)

Perhaps you've not considered this before, but in the moment when you realized that you were a sinner who needed God's rescue, that revelation was a spiritual breakthrough moment for you. That moment didn't come from within you; God revealed it to you.

Read John 16:7-8 in the margin. Who reveals to us our sin and our need for the gospel of grace?

While you might have heard a sermon, listened to a podcast, or hit rock bottom, your realization that you needed God's rescue wasn't your idea. God's Holy Spirit revealed the extent of your sin and called you toward God. Over the years, I've met countless people at the front door of the church who've said to me, "I'm not sure why I'm here. I just woke up this morning and realized that I needed to go to church."

Read 2 Corinthians 5:17 in the margin. Here's an opportunity for a creative moment. In the space provided below, draw a representative picture depicting the concept of this verse.

Therefore, if anyone is in Christ, the new creation has come: The old has gone, the new is here!
(2 Corinthians 5:17 NIV)

When we question whether we deserve God's forgiveness, or when we're afraid that we're not doing enough for God, it's easy to believe the lie that we are not worthy of God's love or freedom. And when we don't feel like we deserve something good, we're more likely to make a case for why we should stay stuck in the bad. When you continue to beat yourself up with your past sins, struggles, and failures, it's as if you're going to the gravesite where Jesus was buried so that you can get your painful past and take it back home with you. Meanwhile, Jesus is saying, "Precious daughter, all that is dead and buried. That's not who you are any more. Stop digging that stuff up."

Is there something from your life before Christ that you need to stop digging back up again and again? If so, what is it?

Let's have a final burial for that. On the tombstone below, write whatever was buried with Christ. Then, review the prayer and fill in the blank:

R I P

Dear God, thank You that I am a new creation in Christ. It's time for me to leave behind once and for all what Jesus already died for on the cross. God, I forever leave buried my guilt, shame and regret over _____

_____.

Jesus died for it, I've been forgiven for it, and I am free from it.

Thank You for that; in Jesus's name. Amen.

Am I saying that you should be in denial of your past? Not at all! Justification begins with the reality that you've sinned. But as we've said, justification means that the price has been paid—as if the sin never happened. When I think back to the mistakes I made before Christ, I like to follow the wisdom, "Look back, but don't stare." The longer that we stare at the past, the more likely we are to get sucked into it. We are not our past; we are the recipients of God's precious promises. Since the gospel is based on God's precious promises, not our performance (sin or mistakes), God's not punishing us for our past, and we don't have to punish ourselves either.

Paul ends Galatians 2 by saying that he does not treat God's grace as meaningless. Unfortunately, that's exactly what Peter did when he stopped eating with the Gentiles because he felt the pressure of the law.

Read Galatians 2:21. What didn't need to happen if keeping the law was enough to make us right with God?

Let that sink in for a moment. Remember, Jesus came to earth to show us what God was like. While He walked among humanity, He was criticized and accused by religious leaders. Not everyone in Jesus's family believed that that He was the Messiah. Jesus allowed Himself to be beaten and crucified by the very people He came to save. Why would He have made such a sacrifice if an adequate system was already in place?

This is where it should get personal for each of us. When we don't see the gospel as enough in our lives, we diminish Jesus's sacrifice. When we wear ourselves out worrying about whether we're reading our Bible enough, serving enough, giving enough, or praying enough like a "good Christian," we treat God's grace as meaningless.

On the other hand, we live fully in the grace of God when we wake up each day and say, "God, I am ready to live for You today." And we live fully in the beautiful grace of God each time we reject the tyranny of rule-keeping and cherish the personal, life-giving relationship we have with God because of what Jesus Christ did for us.

Prayer

God, thank You for my new life in Christ. It doesn't matter if I've been in relationship with You for five minutes or fifty years, You have made me new and are renewing me every single day. I trust that You are at work in my life and I will show up each day and allow the Holy Spirit to keep working in me; in Jesus's name. Amen.

Ah-ha Moment

Did you notice any ah-ha spiritual breakthrough moments in today's study, your prayer time, or your daily activities? If so, record that moment on the final page of this week's study (page 73).

Weekly Breakthrough Reflection Exercise

Each day this week you have been prompted to record on the following page any ah-ha spiritual breakthrough moments you've had in your study, prayer time, or daily activities. Remember, a spiritual breakthrough is an ah-ha moment when we recognize that God is at work within us, receive what He's doing, and respond to it. We want to identify spiritual breakthroughs, both big and small, as a reminder that God is always at work in our lives.

Take time to reflect once more on where you've seen God working in your heart, mind, and life this week, and add any other ah-ha moments on the following page. (*Note*: You can experience more than one breakthrough in a particular category. For example, if there were several moments when you confronted and overcame different fears, each of those moments counts.)

Choose one of your ah-ha moments from the following page and describe it here:

What spiritual breakthrough are you praying for in this study? (Refer to the definition of *spiritual breakthrough* on page 40 before you answer.)

Option: Write a prayer below:

Lightbulb

You gain new understanding about God or yourself.

Describe the moment:

_____

_____

_____

Butterfly

You surrender or let go of a struggle, sin, or stronghold from your past.

Describe the moment:

_____

_____

_____

Rainbow

You find new or renewed hope based on God's promises for your life.

Describe the moment:

_____

_____

_____

Busted Brick Wall

You confront and face up to any kind of fear or worry.

Describe the moment:

_____

_____

_____

Line in the Sand

You realize that a sin, struggle, or stronghold is no longer acceptable.

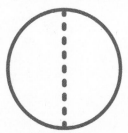

Describe the moment:

_____

_____

_____

Split-the-Rock

You have a supernatural shift in your faith or circumstances after faithfully praying and letting God lead.

Describe the moment:

_____

_____

_____

Video Viewer Guide
WEEK 2

Scriptures: Galatians 2:9, Galatians 2:11-12, Galatians 2:13, Luke 6:43-44a, Luke 6:46,

Acts 10:28, Acts 10:34-35, Matthew 7:3, 5, Galatians 2:20

We can love Jesus and still make _____.

There's a difference between a hypocrite who _____ and a hypocrite who _____,

Keep your _____ on your own Hula-Hoop.

Freedom Principle #2

A relationship with God means that we _____ from Him rather than follow _____ for Him.

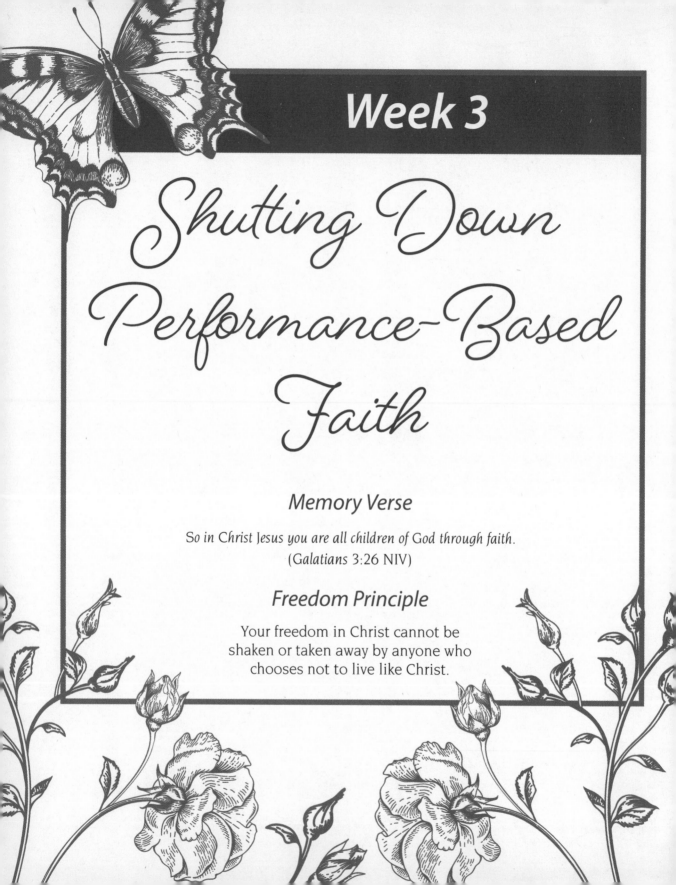

Shutting Down Performance-Based Faith

Memory Verse

So in Christ Jesus you are all children of God through faith.
(Galatians 3:26 NIV)

Freedom Principle

Your freedom in Christ cannot be
shaken or taken away by anyone who
chooses not to live like Christ.

My daughter, Sami, wanted to make fancy-looking Italian pork chops with stuffing. Since she was cooking for her boyfriend on a special occasion, she followed each detail meticulously to make sure that nothing went wrong. When the timer went off, Sami immediately took the dish out of the oven. She noticed that the meat wasn't fully cooked in the center, so she put it back in the oven for a few minutes. But even after that, the meat still wasn't cooked all the way through. That's when she called me in tears: "Mom, he's almost here, and I think that dinner is ruined. I followed the directions, but it's not turning out like it's supposed to."

Eventually, the meat was cooked through. However, the stuffing was overcooked, burned. My daughter took one bite of her meal and burst into tears.

When she called me again later that night to tell me about the disastrous meal, she shared the grace-filled words that her boyfriend had said as she cried at the table. He said to my beautiful girl: "It's okay, honey. You're tried. We can salvage the night by getting pizza."

Perhaps God is saying to you today, "I know that you want to please me, but trying to follow the rules just right is breaking your heart. You can stop trying so hard. You don't need to stress yourself out trying to live the perfect Christian life like following a recipe. Our relationship is enough."

In our study this week, Paul expands upon the reasons why the law wasn't the remedy that our hearts needed. Like a recipe, the law itself is a good thing; but because of the people's sin, following the law didn't guarantee perfection. You'll see the connections between the old covenant and the new covenant and why the law was needed between them. Later in the week, we'll study the vision Paul cast on a topic that our world needs now more than ever: *unity*.

Day 1: Step One: Stop Following the Recipe

Most of us have a recipe of rules for the Christian life based on what we think a good Christian looks like. Our recipes may include a few different ingredients depending on our particular denomination. Here's what my Christian-life recipe looked like for many years:

Big Idea

A relationship with God is much more fulfilling than following a recipe of rules.

- 1 c weekly church attendance
- 1 c daily Bible study
- 1 c volunteering (or 2 c if pressured to do more)
- 1 c Bible study group (sometimes a seasonal ingredient)
- 1 c offering (or a dash if money is tight)

- 1 c prayer (add more if you gossip, lie, or accidently swear)
- 1 c good intentions

Directions: Mix together each week on your calendar. For consistency, each ingredient must be mixed in each week, even if you're sick. Substitute guilt for any missing ingredients. Season with "Hallelujah," "Amen," "Won't He do it?" or any other favorite Christian cliché. Pour generous amounts of worship music over the top to cover anything that might be outdated or less than fresh. Serve with a Sunday smile.

What's your recipe for the Christian life? Write it below. (You don't have to fill in all the blanks.)

1 c _____

1 c _____

1 c _____

1 c _____

1 c _____

Directions:

For years, I felt confident about my recipe of rules. As long as I mixed together the ingredients consistently, I relished the idea that my actions made God feel good about me. That was important to me.

However, in those seasons when my kids didn't sleep at night, when I worked long hours and was too tired to read my Bible, or when I was depressed and didn't feel like praying, this recipe felt like grumpy restauranteur Gordon Ramsay calling me names like "slacker" or "bad Christian." There's nothing that a Jesus-girl is afraid of more than being called a bad Christian. Wait, there is something worse: feeling like I was failing God.

My spiritual breakthrough came during a wilderness season of my life when an addiction issue surfaced within our family. As the crisis intensified, there were days when I could barely crawl out of bed, much less mix up my recipe. On one desperate day in my prayer closet, I cried out, "God, change me." That's when I stopped putting my faith in my recipe as a formula for faith and began to look more to God Himself for transformation. Though the recipe I shared is still a part of my life, now it's not a formula but a *guide* meant only to help align me with God's heart—so that H*e* can fuel me with peace and power.

Is your Christian-life "recipe" a formula or a guide? Explain.

In the first verses of Galatians 3, we see that Paul asks a firestorm of questions of his audience.

Read Galatians 3:1-5. Write below all of the questions Paul asks in these verses:

You're going to answer these questions for yourself at the end of today's study. But first, let's learn why Paul had so many questions.

In verse 1, Paul begins by calling the Galatians *foolish*. That's awkward. Why would he use a word like that? The Bible has a lot to say about communicating with each other with kindness. Today, calling someone a fool is similar to calling someone stupid. However, Paul wasn't calling the Galatians stupid. The Greek word for *foolish* that Paul used is *anoétos*,[1] which means "not thinking through a matter, or unwise." He wanted them to stop and think not only about what they were doing, but also about why they were doing it.

Paul appealed to the memory of their salvation experience. While it's not wise to base our faith on our emotions or experience, our experience is a part of our faith journey. It's as if Paul was saying, "Come on, you guys. You heard the gospel. You knew what you were doing when you accepted Jesus Christ. Why are you letting others talk you out of what you've experienced and what you believe?"

Paul witnessed the Holy Spirit moving in their hearts, and they believed the gospel for themselves. No one forced them to say "yes" or gave them a post-salvation list of to-do's after Paul preached. But they began to question their salvation experience when the Judaizers showed up.

Paul wasn't the only one to call believers foolish. Jesus used the same language after His resurrection as he was walking incognito with two people on the road to Emmaus (Luke 24:25). Jesus called the two men foolish because although they were His followers, they had questioned His teachings and whether He was the Messiah. After Jesus confronted them, He spent the rest of their journey to Emmaus teaching them again from what the prophets had said about the Messiah. Even Jesus had to repeat His teachings, not because there was anything wrong with His previous teachings, but because His followers had a problem listening and believing.

Following Jesus's example in Luke 24:27, Paul walked the Galatians through their salvation experience. The second question He asked was if they received the Holy Spirit because they had obeyed the law.

According to Galatians 3:2, why does the Holy Spirit indwell believers?

Read Romans 8:10-11, and list what the Holy Spirit does in the life of a believer:

Write verse 11 below:

What does this verse mean to you?

What a gift we've been given that the Holy Spirit lives within us! Romans 8:11 contains one of the most powerful points of hope for me, a reforming rule-follower. Here's what is true: following the rules never gives us life. It might provide some satisfaction and a feeling of superiority. But there's

Extra Insight

"The law has the power to show us that we are not righteous; but it cannot give us the power to be righteous."[2]

always the fear that we've got to keep up with rule-following. It's all on us. But Romans 8:11 speaks such powerful truth to you and me. We're the recipients of an indwelling Spirit who does for us what we can't do on our own.

Take a moment to answer these paraphrases of the questions that Paul posed in Galatians 3:1-5.

1. **Who has talked you into questioning the wholeness or validity of your faith, either in the past or present? What are you learning or remembering now to restore your confidence in what you believe? (v. 1)**

2. **Did you receive the Holy Spirit by doing all the right things or because you believed in what Jesus did for you? (v. 2)**

3. **Are you trying to become perfect by your own effort? Does your faith seem more like a recipe/formula or a guide? (v. 3)**

4. **Being a follower of Christ isn't without difficulty. What hard times or difficult moments have you experienced as the result of being a Christ follower? How have those times impacted your beliefs about who God is? (v. 4)**

Ah-ha Moment

Did you notice any ah-ha spiritual breakthrough moments in today's study, your prayer time, or your daily activities? If so, record that moment on the final page of this week's study (page 107).

5. **How have you seen God's Holy Spirit at work in your life? How have you been transformed? What are the places in your attitudes, beliefs, or behaviors where you suspect you're trying to do the work that only God can do? (v. 5)**

6. **What is the most important thing you need to remember or do in light of today's lesson?**

Whether you've been a believer for a long time or you're new to a relationship with Christ, Paul's words in Galatians 3:1-5 remind us that we must be vigilant in *thinking about our thinking*. We have to be clear about what our beliefs are so that we can live them out and be aware of them when others pressure us to change our beliefs.

If you're like me, it's easy to pull out a spiritual recipe card when you're feeling afraid or insecure in your relationship with God. Often, it's the influence of others that can plant those seeds of insecurity. For me, the best way to take the focus off others and my fears is to practice seeing God at work. This is why I developed the six categories of spiritual breakthrough moments to use in my life—and now I'm sharing them with you.

Keep your eyes open to where you see God at work in your heart, mind, and life. Trust that He is leading you to freedom as you focus on Him.

Prayer

God, thank You for the power of Your Holy Spirit at work within me. Thank You for the life that the Spirit brings to me. Remind me that I do not need to live a recipe of rules because a relationship with You is much more fulfilling; in Jesus's name. Amen.

Day 2: God's Perfect Promise

When my kids were little, they loved to visit the local zoo. We went often and my little girls never lost their enthusiasm for petting the animals, looking at the fish, or watching to see if the monkeys were swinging from branch to branch. A few days before each visit, they would look up at me and say, "Mom, we're still going to the zoo, right? Remember, you promised."

They loved the zoo, so they worried that something would keep me from fulfilling my promise to them. Since they couldn't get themselves to the zoo on their own, they had to learn how to trust and believe that I would do what I said that I was going to do.

In today's lesson, Paul teaches us about covenant and a very important lesson that Abraham models for us. Specifically, we will look at three covenants in the Bible that serve different purposes but work together with regard to our eternal relationship with God.

Abrahamic Covenant

Paul begins with the covenant between God and Abraham in the Old Testament. Abraham was a Semite, a descendant of Shem, one of Noah's sons. One day, God spoke to seventy-five-year old Abraham, who at first was called Abram. He called Abram to leave his family's home and travel to Canaan, a land that God would give to Abram's descendants (Genesis 12:1).

> **Read Galatians 3:6-9 and write verse 6 below.**

> **Read Genesis 15:6 and Romans 4:9-10 in the margin. Why was Abram declared righteous? Did this happen before or after he was circumcised?**

Last week, we learned in Galatians 2:16 that being declared righteous means justification, or God's declaration of innocence according to His holy standard. Abram was declared righteous. He believed God, and that was enough. As one source states, "He didn't do anything; he believed something."[4] Abram didn't pray a prayer. He didn't light any candles or make

Big Idea

When God makes a promise, He doesn't need our help to keep it.

Extra Insight

Commentary on Galatians 3:6:

"If, therefore, the great patriarch Abraham was declared righteous on account of his faith (and not because he was circumcised), why did the Galatians need to become circumcised?"[3]

Abram believed the LORD, and he credited it to him as righteousness.
(Genesis 15:6 NIV)

---

[9]We have been saying that Abraham's faith was credited to him as righteousness. [10]Under what circumstances was it credited? Was it after he was circumcised, or before? It was not after, but before!
(Romans 4:9-10 NIV)

promises to not fall behind on his daily Bible study time. He believed God, and God credited him righteousness.

> **Reflect on Abram's belief alone, without any other requirements. Is there a place in your life that you need to choose to believe God without making it more complicated? Explain your response.**

When Abram showed up in Canaan, there were already people living there. So it was a demonstration of extraordinary faith for Abram to believe that God would give him, a foreigner and childless man, all that land for his future descendants. Even more amazing is there's no indication in Scripture that Abram grew up knowing anything about God. It's more likely that he was surrounded by pagan gods of all types. Let's face it, many of us who grew up in the church have trouble holding on to God's promises, but Abram believed based on what God told him.

Here's where the covenant comes in. In Genesis 15:8, Abram asks about God's promise to give him a son. Many childless years had passed, and rather than display doubt, Abram calls upon God for help and confirmation.

> **Read Genesis 15:9-18, and put the statements in numerical order from 1-7.**
>
> A ___ God tells Abram that he will die in peace at an old age.
>
> B. ___ God commands Abram to gather a young heifer, goat, ram, turtle dove, and pigeon.
>
> C. ___ God made a covenant with Abram promising to give his descendants the land he currently occupied.
>
> D. ___ God tells Abram that his future descendants will be enslaved for 400 years.
>
> E. ___ Abram killed the animals and cut them in half, except for the dove and pigeon.
>
> F. ___ Abram fell into a deep sleep.
>
> G. ___ Abram saw a smoking firepot and flaming torch pass through the animal halves.

Answers: A. 5, B. 1, C. 7, D. 4, E. 2, F. 3, G. 6

In our modern context, making an agreement with someone looks a lot like a handshake, signing a contract, or clicking a box online. However, God tells Abram to gather some animals and prepare them. Depending on how you feel about animals, this might be offensive to you. In ancient times, however, this was the way that an agreement was ratified or accepted. As one source explains, "Both parties to the covenant were supposed to walk between the slain animals, signaling that if either one broke their side of the agreement, he would suffer a fate like that of the animals."[5]

After Abram prepared the animals, God put Abram to sleep, which might remind us of when God put Adam to sleep in order to create Eve (Genesis 2:21). While Abram was asleep, God gave him insight into the future of his family, even though Abram did not yet have any children. God told of the Israelites' future years of slavery and even their leaving Egypt with great wealth. Abram received notice of all these blessings and, best of all, he was not doing anything other than staring at the back of his eyelids while God made these promises.

Next, Abram saw a smoking firepot and flaming torch pass through the divided carcasses. Commentators suggest these symbolize different aspects of God's character. One scholar proposes that the smoke represented God's mysteriousness and the flame God's power.[6]

The Abrahamic covenant is a symbol of how God promises us good things, not because He wants us to earn them, but because He is a good God. Abraham reminds us that believing God's promises is enough. Period.

How does God's covenant with Abraham reflect the gospel of grace as it relates to us?

Last week, we learned about the law as well as the new covenant through Jesus. That was a lot of information, so it's good that we have an opportunity to apply what we learned in our lesson today as Paul again discusses the law in Galatians 3. This time he teaches his audience about the relationship between God's promise and the law that God gave to Moses.

Read Galatians 3:17-18. Was God's promise to Abraham canceled when Moses gave God's law to the Israelites? Explain your answer.

Extra Insight

"…before he came to faith,…Paul never really lived for God. He was being very moral and good—but it was all for Paul, never for God."[7]

Complete the following:

Even though God gave the Israelites the law, it did not invalidate God's p_____ to Abraham.

Read Galatians 3:19. Why was the law given?

The big picture takeaway is that when God gave the law to Moses, He was not changing the terms of His promise to Abraham and his descendants.

As I reflect on the relationship between the Abrahamic, Mosaic, and new covenants, I'm reminded of a relay race. Of course, it has its limitations, as all analogies do. But it illustrates how, in a sense, each covenant "hands off" to the next one like an inbound runner passing the baton to the outgoing runner. Neither the covenant with Abram nor the one with Israel through Moses is going to run the full race on its own. Yet, rather than picking up where the previous covenant left off, we might think of the next covenant or "runner" as more of an extension, carrying it further—which simply means that one covenant is not revoked when a new one is instituted. God wants us not only to receive the covenant extended to us, but also to run the race in the grace that He has given to us (Philippians 3:14).

The Relay of the Covenants

The diagram on the following page shows the relay relationship between the three covenants.

Look up each Scripture reference on the folliwing page and choose from the Word Bank to fill in the blanks.

Even though the Abrahamic and Mosaic covenants seemed to be concerned with only the Jewish people, God gave Abraham a taste of His greater divine vision in Genesis 12:3.

Reread Genesis 12:3 and Galatians 3:8. Write again who would be blessed through Abraham:

ABRAHAMIC COVENANT

God promised Abraham that all

_____ would be blessed

through him. (Galatians 3:8; Genesis 12:3)

Abraham _____ God

and it was credited to him as

_____ .

(Galatians 3:6, Genesis 15:6)

God's promise to Abraham could not be

_____.

(Galatians 3:15-17)

Word Bank:
nations, blood of Christ, set aside,
the coming of the child, believed,
put their faith in God, new covenant,
sins, righteousness

MOSAIC COVENANT

The law was given alongside the

promise to show the people their

_____. (Galatians 3:19)

The law was designed to last only until

_____ who

was promised. (Galatians 3:19)

NEW COVENANT (CHRIST)

1 Corinthians 11:25 explains the basis of
the new covenant. What is it?

_____ of _____

According to Galatians 3:7, the real

children of Abraham are those who

_____

_____

Answers: Abrahamic covenant:
nations, believed, righteousness,
set aside;
Mosaic covenant: sins, the
coming of the child;
new covenant: blood of Christ,
put their faith in God.

Ah-ha Moment

Did you notice any ah-ha spiritual breakthrough moments in today's study, your prayer time, or your daily activities? If so, record that moment on the final page of this week's study (page 107).

Now read Galatians 3:9. What do those who put their faith in Christ share with Abraham?

As believers, we are children of a God who has promised us good things— again, not because we have any ability to gain those good things on our own, but because God is a good God.

My prayer is that you are inspired by Abraham's simple faith. He believed God. I also pray that you see the divinely ordered progression—from God's promises to Abraham, to the law's role in exposing that we can't be righteous on our own, to Jesus's new covenant, making it possible for all of us to experience God's promises and goodness.

As you reflect on today's study, what is a takeaway that you want to remember from what you've learned?

Prayer

God, thank You for the promise that You gave Abraham long ago that all the nations and people of the world would be blessed through him. And thank You for Your faithfulness in sending Jesus to fulfill that promise so that I could have a relationship with You; in Jesus's name. Amen.

Day 3: Three Fabulous Freedoms

Big Idea

Your freedom in Christ cannot be shaken or taken away!

Freedom is God's dream for you...

Freedom from the prison of your pain.
Freedom from the prison of your problems.
Freedom from the prison of your past.
Freedom from whatever it is that makes you feel afraid or feel like a failure.

Jesus came and died to so that you could experience eternal freedom from sin as well as freedom from wherever you come from or whatever you've been through.

One writer put it like this: "God is committed to freeing His children from every present lie, snare, and bondage."[8] Here's the good news: God has already won your freedom! He did that through Christ. However, do you know what you've been freed from? Do you truly believe that you can be free?

On January 1, 1863, President Abraham Lincoln signed the Emancipation Proclamation, freeing enslaved people. However, in Texas, the slaves didn't know that they had been freed. It wasn't until the spring of 1865 when federal troops arrived in Galveston, Texas, that the slaves found out they'd been freed over two years before.[9] It's one thing to wake up each day and know that you are enslaved, but to wake up each day and not know that you are actually free is a tragedy.

In John 8:36, Jesus says to those who believe in Him: "So if the Son sets you free, you are truly free." Too many of us wake up each day worried that we aren't really free. Perhaps that's why we believe that jumping through religious hoops will fill the places where we feel like we're failing God. The good news is that we *have* been set free, and as we know God more, He leads us toward a life free from fear and fully alive.

If that kind of freedom feels far away, don't give up! While you might feel like a caterpillar that has given up hope of change, waiting in the dark inside a chrysalis, God is still at work in your life. Could it be that wherever you feel stuck or trapped is the very place where God's transformation is happening in your life?

In today's lesson, we will learn about three types of freedom made possible by the gospel of grace. In John 8:32, Jesus declares, "And you will know the truth, and the truth will set you free." Freedom must be supported by truth or it isn't real freedom. Jesus is the key to your freedom from whatever prison you find yourself in; Jesus is the key to your breakthrough.

Unfortunately, not every believer experiences this freedom. Far too many Christians cling to their legalism wheels, refusing to allow God's perfect promises to work in their lives so that they experience God's adventure of purpose.

As we continue in Galatians 3, Paul asks an important question in verse 21 that leads to a revelation not only for His Galatian audience but also for us: "Is there a conflict, then, between God's law and God's promises?" In other words, is there a tension between God's holy standards for living and God's freely given promises that depend not on our actions but on His faithfulness? Paul's answer is no!

Here's Galatians 3:21-22 in *The Message*, which expands on why there is no conflict:

If such is the case, is the law, then, an anti-promise, a negation of God's will for us? Not at all. Its purpose was to make obvious to everyone that we are, in ourselves, out of right relationship with God, and therefore to show us the futility of devising some religious system for getting by our own efforts what we can only get by waiting in faith for God to complete his promise. For if any kind of rule-keeping had power to create life in us, we would certainly have gotten it by this time.

(Galatians 3:21-22 MSG)

Summarize below the main points of these verses:

The law directed people's actions but couldn't change their hearts and minds, and the law certainly didn't have power to help them overcome the fear, self-centeredness, pride, and more that kept them in violation of the law. Of course, someone could endeavor to follow the law and feel a sense of satisfaction or even superiority, but that feeling would only last until the next moment when they had to keep the next law. Can you relate? That's why I love the last line of Galatians 3:22 in *The Message*, which says, "For if any kind of rule-keeping had the power to create life in us, we would have certainly have gotten it by this time."

So letting your sinful nature control your mind leads to death. But letting the Spirit control your mind leads to life and peace.

(Romans 8:6)

Read Romans 8:6 in the margin. What are the two things that we experience in the new covenant that trying to follow rules can't give us?

L _____ and P _____

Every now and then a debate arises about whether Christians today should read the Old Testament. Some argue that since Jesus fulfilled the law and we're the recipients of the new covenant, then the Old Testament is irrelevant. Like most biblical scholars, I do not agree. Besides the fact that the gospel and new covenant are the fulfillment of the Old Testament promises (which means that both the Old and New Testaments tell the full story of God's redemption plan), the stories that we read in the Old Testament about people whose hearts and minds are just like ours show us why we all need the gospel. When I read the Old Testament, I am reminded of two important things:

1. God's love for us has never changed.
2. Our love for sin hasn't changed either.

When we read the Old Testament, we find some really peculiar laws in Leviticus, such as, "Do not wear clothing woven from two different kinds of thread" (Leviticus 19:19). While some laws cause confusion and conflict related to social issues today, others offer deep and rich wisdom that transcends human history.

In Galatians 3:23-25, Paul uses a cultural analogy to describe the role of the law in the time between Abraham and the new covenant.

Read Galatians 3:23-25. What was the role that the law fulfilled?

Paul writes that the Israelites were kept in custody by the law. He describes the law as a temporary guardian. The Greek word for guardian is *paidagógos*,[10] which describes a slave owned by the family who was entrusted with tutoring the children as well as disciplining them.[11] One commentary adds this insight to Paul's analogy:

> In any case that job lasted only until the children reached the age of maturity. Then his responsibility was at an end. Now, Paul insists that "faith came" and brought our time with the law to an end since it pointed to Christ, who alone can set us right with God.[12]

While our lives aren't influenced by all of the Jewish laws today, we are influenced by our own internal laws of self-righteousness ("I must do X to find favor with God"), which often lead us away from God's best. Just as the law demonstrates how far our hearts are from God, so the gospel guarantees that Christ draws us near through a personal relationship with Him.

Let's end our lesson today by celebrating God's life-giving promises of freedom for our lives! We're defining freedom in Christ as *living free from fear and fully alive with joy and purpose*. And our freedom in Christ cannot be shaken or taken away by anyone who chooses not to live like Christ. When we're living fully in that confidence, we're free from the prison of sin and the soul-draining consequences of being a prisoner.

Read the verses on the following pages and answer the questions that follow. At the end of today's lesson, there is a final prayer exercise that incorporates all of these insights.

1. Freedom from Fear

But Jesus spoke to them at once. "Don't be afraid," he said. "Take courage! I am here!"

(Mark 6:50)

God is love...Such love has no fear, because perfect love expels all fear. If we are afraid, it is for fear of punishment, and this shows that we have not fully experienced his perfect love.

(1 John 4:16b, 18)

For God has not given us a spirit of fear and timidity, but of power, love, and self-discipline.

(2 Timothy 1:7)

Why can you have freedom from fear?

What fears does the gospel of grace give you freedom over today?

Which verse connects most strongly with you today and why?

2. Freedom from Self-Destruction
   (pride, ego, self-centeredness, self-sabatage)

I will walk in freedom,
   for I have devoted myself to your commandments.
                    (Psalm 119:45)

Oh, what a miserable person I am! Who will free me from this life that is dominated by sin and death? Thank God! The answer is in Jesus Christ our Lord.

(Romans 7:24-25a)

For the Lord is the Spirit, and wherever the Spirit of the Lord is, there is freedom.

(2 Corinthians 3:17)

How can you experience freedom from self-destruction?

Why do you need freedom from self-destruction?

Which verse connects most strongly with you today and why?

3. Freedom from Death

25 Jesus told her, "I am the resurrection and the life. Anyone who believes in me will live, even after dying. 26 Everyone who lives in me and believes in me will never ever die."

(John 11:25-26)

And because you belong to him, the power of the life-giving Spirit has freed you from the power of sin that leads to death.

(Romans 8:2)

14 Because God's children are human beings—made of flesh and blood—the Son also became flesh and blood. For only as a human being could he die, and only by dying could he break the power of the devil, who had the power of death. 15 Only in this way could he set free all who have lived their lives as slaves to the fear of dying.

(Hebrews 2:14-15)

How can you experience freedom from the fear of death?

When we think about death, we consider our mortality, but we also think about those we love. How does it comfort you knowing that the gospel can bring freedom from death not only for you but also for those you care about?

Ah-ha Moment

Did you notice any ah-ha spiritual breakthrough moments in today's study, your prayer time, or your daily activities? If so, record that moment on the final page of this week's study (page 107).

Which verse connects most strongly with you today and why?

As we study Galatians 5 and 6 in future lessons, you'll learn more verses about your freedom in Christ. For now, my prayer is that the verses you've read will remind you of the great freedom in Christ that is yours. I don't know where you may feel stuck, stalled, or unsettled in your faith, but my hope is that you allow God's truth to address the questions you've been asking.

Prayer

Dear God, today I needed to be reminded that I am free from _____

_____. Even when it doesn't seem like it's true, You've

given me freedom. So God, when I feel closed in or captive by feelings like

_____ or thoughts like _____

_____, remind me of the verse that says, "_____

_____

_____."

(write a verse you want to remember here), so that I can replace my thoughts with Your truth; in Jesus's name. Amen.

Day 4: The Gospel Power of Unity

Big Idea

The gospel makes it possible for us to stand together!

During the Olympic opening ceremonies, I love watching the different countries of the world as they march into the stadium wearing coordinating uniforms under their country's flag. I remember the special moment during the 2016 Rio Olympics when Team USA marched in led by multiple gold-medal winner Michael Phelps carrying the United States flag. While I enjoyed watching the other countries, a warm and lovely sensation spread over me as I looked at Team USA on the screen. They were *my* team. As I watched them compete, I cheered and screamed for them as if I was their teammate.

The Olympics remind us of the very best of what it means to be part of a team. Whether you've played on a team or have cheered someone on, there's a powerful sense of connection that is a part of that community experience.

Unfortunately, because of long-standing and deep divides in our country along political, racial, and social lines, often we don't feel like we're Team USA. Those same divides tend to follow us into our weekend church services as well. But those divisions are not how the church is supposed to be.

After imploring the Galatians to break up with their pursuit of righteousness through the law, Paul uses the final verses of chapter 3 to cast a vision of the greatest relational blessing the gospel has to offer us here on earth: unity.

I define unity as *a gathering of imperfect people passionately committed to something greater than themselves.* Unity is powerful because our human nature is to reject our differences and tear each other down. Lucky for us, the gospel of grace recognizes our shortcomings as human beings. As believers, we're united by the gospel that frees us to stand together and share Jesus's message with the world.

Reread the definition of unity in the preceding paragraph. When was the last time you felt a sense of unity or togetherness with your Bible study group, social/volunteer organization, or church?

What contributed to that sense of unity?

In Galatians 3:26-29, Paul lays out how the gospel unifies us. As you read the verses, pay attention to the repetition of the word "all."

Read Galatians 3:26-29 and answer the following questions:

What makes us children of God? (v. 26)

When we are united with Christ, baptism is like we are putting on new _____. (v. 27)

What is the main message of verse 28?

As heirs of Christ, to what are we entitled? (v. 29)

*All peoples on earth
will be blessed
through you.*
(Genesis 12:3b NIV)

In Genesis 12:3 (in the margin), God tells Abraham that all peoples on earth will be blessed through him, and in Galatians 3 Paul explains how the "relay race" of the three covenants culminates in Christ, so that God's people who lived long ago, those who lived under the law until Christ, and all who believe in Christ—which includes us—are the true children of Abraham.

What did Paul mean by saying that baptism is like putting on new clothes? First, baptism wasn't intended to be a substitute for circumcision. Additonally, baptism wasn't intended to be an act of salvation; rather, water immersion was a symbolic picture of putting on the character of Christ.

Read Colossians 3:12-14. What are the "clothing" characteristics that believers should wear?

How do these qualities support an individual's contribution toward unity with other believers?

Both Galatians 3:26-29 and Colossians 3:12-14 use the image of "putting on" or "clothing ourselves" as a spiritual metaphor. Galatians 3:26-29 suggests that we're clothed with Christ through baptism, reflecting the inner transformation of the Holy Spirit, while Colossians 3:12-14 uses the language that we're "putting on" clothing, representing our reponse to the Spirit's work in us. As we choose to respond to what God is doing, our behaviors should reflect the character of Christ within us; and the result should be unity with other like-minded believers.

In the left column, list the characteristics of Christ that you feel you're currently wearing, and in the right column, list the ones

you would like to put on more often in response to the Spirit's work in you:

I'm currently wearing: I would like to put on more often:

Whenever there is conflict, there are always two sides. However, you are only in control of *your* actions and attitudes. So, consider any conflicts that you might be having with other believers in your life. Could there be any connections between the conflict and the characteristics you need to wear more often? Write your thoughts below:

In verse 28, Paul explains how the gospel breaks down the walls of culture, class, and gender[13] that we often erect out of pride or superiority. In Paul's day, the gospel meant that Gentiles, women, and slaves were now on the same level as the men and religious leaders. Imagine the beautiful scandal in that! It would be like a server at a country club strolling into the main dining area, taking a seat at the best table, and being served as if he or she was a top member of the club. The gospel means that every believer is a top member in God's kingdom.

When Paul says that we're all one in Christ, does that mean we're to ignore our differences? Not at all! When it comes to the gospel, Paul teaches that everyone is an equal heir to the promises of God. Furthermore, since we are all heirs to the promises of God, we're to treat each other as equal heirs. There's no room, space, or place for jealousy, pride, hatred, or superiority because all of us are recipients of God's precious promises.

If that's the case, then shouldn't that be cause for celebration and true community with one another? Shouldn't the gospel be powerful enough in our lives to bind us together as brothers and sisters in Christ? You'd think so, but clearly that's not the case.

Why do you think Christians have always struggled and continue to struggle with unity despite the fact that we say the gospel is the center of our faith? (There's no wrong answer; just give your opinion.)

Throughout the history of the church, division has defined us. This is exactly the opposite of what Jesus prayed for us right before He went to the cross.

Read John 17:20-23. Write verse 20, and then summarize Jesus's prayer in these four verses:

Extra Insight

"Paul does not call believers to be unified. Instead, we are unified in Christ and we are to maintain the unity that is already ours."[14]

Jesus was praying not only for His disciples and followers, but also for me, you, and anyone else who would follow Him in the future. Jesus's final prayer was for unity. The gospel has united us, but it's our choice whether we will extend our hands to the brothers and sisters in Christ around us and live united—not in spite of our differences, but as a way of embracing our differences.

Could it be that in the midst of all the divisions we have as believers, we have an extraordinary opportunity to show the world—especially those who are far from God—what the gospel looks like through our unity? Imagine how powerful that could be! Unity is the vehicle that transports the gospel to the world. In fact, John 17:23 suggests that our unity can be our most effective evangelism vehicle in a world defined by division.

The word *unity* itself can be an acronym for the elements that help us to fulfill Jesus's prayer.

Read and complete the following:

Unique
When we combine our unique strengths, we create synergy and momentum.

Read 1 Corinthians 12:12-14. We are all one in Christ, but we are made of up of different p_____.

Numbers
When we unify, God multiplies our numbers.

Read Acts 2:46-47. What happened as a result of the believers coming together?

Inspiration
When we agree that the gospel is our top focus, we find inspiration for a united faith.

Read Galatians 3:26. What unites us as believers?

Team
When we live according to "One for all and all for the One," we are united as a team.

Read Acts 2:42-44. What kind of unity is described in these verses?

You
When you choose passionate commitment to the gospel and live as one with other believers, you will be united in the Spirit.

Read Ephesians 4:3-6. How does "make every effort" apply to your life when it comes to your commitment to being unified with other believers in your community of faith?

Extra Insights

"As Christians, we have a solution, because our oneness in Christ gives us the position and power to make a statement to the world about the wonder of our faith. The very thing the world needs we have, but because we are so much like the world, the world does not know that we have it."[15]

How can we be a part of answering Jesus's prayer for unity in John 17? We must be *committed* to unity. It isn't easy, especially when others aren't as focused on the gospel. However, each of us can make a commitment to live in unity and trust God to deal with those who divide. And we can remember

Ah-ha Moment

Did you notice any ah-ha spiritual breakthrough moments in today's study, your prayer time, or your daily activities? If so, record that moment on the final page of this week's study (page 107).

that our freedom in Christ cannot be shaken or taken by anyone who chooses not to live like Christ. So, let's choose to be committed to unity, leaving the outcomes to God.

Prayer

God, I love that Jesus prayed for unity for all believers, both then and now. While I do not have control over others or outcomes, I can be committed to championing unity in my life. I choose to clothe myself in Christ and the qualities that reflect Christ. And in those times when it's hard for me to join with other believers, I won't give up on unity but will allow Your Spirit to work in me; in Jesus's name. Amen.

Day 5: All of God's Children

Big Idea

God cares about all of His children, and so should we.

This week we've considered Paul's reminders to the Galatians about the gospel, highlighting or celebrating their oneness in Christ. His words remind us that we are all children of God, which provides an opportunity for us to discuss an important question for all Christians today: *Are we truly seeing every believer as an equal heir to God's promises?*

Since Paul's priority was the gospel, he was not writing about social issues or calling for a cultural revolution. Again, he kept the gospel as his main focus. Yet, Paul surely knew that as the gospel's power began to bring down the walls of divisions between believers, their unity would overflow into the world.

Unfortunately, within the church the roots of division can be traced back to our inability to navigate our differences. We don't understand what makes us different, we may refuse to acknowledge our differences, or we're unwilling to listen to those who live differently than we do. As painful as it is to acknowledge this enduring reality, the good news of the gospel is that our differences don't have to create division.

As we saw yesterday, before dying for all of humanity, Jesus prayed that our perfect unity as believers would be the evidence to the world that the gospel transcends differences and brings people together (John 17:23).

I've shared previously that for many years, I served as the only black staff member at my large, nearly all-Caucasian church. One of the most helpful examples that I watched during my years on staff was my senior pastor's commitment to having lunch with the black pastors in our community several

times a month. As those pastors gathered, they shared their lives together like the Acts 2 community of believers. Those pastoral lunches also created opportunities for real conversation, breaking down barriers that divided black pastors and white pastors. Eventually, our church began partnerships with black churches that still exist today, and together our unified presence and witness in the community is making a lasting and positive impact for eternity.

Talking about our differences, especially when it concerns our different colors and cultures, isn't easy. I know that I'm writing this study for people of all colors and cultures. I also know that today's lesson is a broad overview on a very complicated topic. However, we want to establish a foundation that creates opportunities for us to embrace the same posture as the Acts 2 community that saw incredible growth (Acts 2:47).

As we enter into today's topic, what might be difficult or uncomfortable for you when it comes to talking about race and other differences that divide us?

If you're doing this study with a group, what concerns (if any) do you have about your group conversation?

In light of Paul's teachings on how the gospel makes it possible for us to stand together as children of God, we're going to look at three points that help us to see that our differences do not distract from our unity but actually equip us to share the gospel more effectively. Let's dive in.

1. Jesus's prayer for our unity in diversity reflects the nature of God.

Within God's very nature is diversity, described as the *Trinity*. While the word *Trinity* isn't a word specifically mentioned in the Bible, the doctrine of the Trinity states "that there is one God who eternally exists as three distinct Persons—the Father, Son, and Holy Spirit. Stated differently, God is one in essence and three in person."[16]

One of the most well-known references to the Trinity occurs in Matthew 28:19, where Jesus issues the Great Commission, instructing His followers to make disciples of all nations and baptize them in the name of the Father, Son, and Holy Spirit.

In the Trinity, we see the love and cooperation of the three persons of the Godhead toward each other. In His prayer in John 14:15-17, Jesus refers several times to unique activities of God the Father and God the Holy Spirit that combine for a unified purpose.

> **In John 14:15-17, what are the roles of the three persons of the Trinity?**
>
> **Jesus asks His disciples to obey His _____. (v. 15)**
>
> **God the Father will send the _____, who will never leave us. (v. 16)**
>
> **The Holy Spirit leads us into all _____. (v. 17)**

Extra Insight

To engage in more diverse worship experiences, consider attending a church that is culturally different or watch a service online.

Ultimately, God's triune nature models for us how to live in unity and celebrate our differences. As one source notes, "This [triune] family is the original pattern from which God creates all the families of earth with their unity and diversity."[17]

When it comes to diversity within the church, the Trinity shows us that we can be distinct and yet work together. The Trinity demonstrates mutual submission, which we can emulate by recognizing any unrecognized bias or harmful stereotypes that may prevent people who look or live differently than we do from hearing the gospel message or joining our church community.

2. God purposefully introduced different colors and cultures into the world.

In the story of Creation in Genesis 1, we read that God created different types of animals, plants, and landscapes. Then in verse 26, we read that God created human beings in His diverse image. Note what God says: "Let *us* make human beings in *our* image, to be like *us*" (emphasis added). Here we see another reference to a Triune God who would reflect God's diversity in humanity. In other words, "Like the Trinity, humanity has unity in diversity. . . so every human reflects the unity of God."[18]

Unfortunately, sin entered the world, and eventually humanity's wickedness resulted in God destroying every living thing except for Noah, his family, and the animals that God instructed Noah to bring aboard the boat that would keep them safe (Genesis 7). After the flood, God blessed Noah and his sons, telling them to be fruitful and multiply throughout the earth (Genesis 9:1). Yet at the beginning of Genesis 11, we see that the people were settled near Babylon and had come up with a new group project.

Read Genesis 11:1. What did all the people in the world share?

In Genesis 11:7, God decides to make it impossible for the people to understand each other. What does He do?

In verse 8, the people scatter all over world. Who causes them to scatter?

The story of the tower of Babel has been interpreted in different ways. Some scholars believe that God punished humans for wanting to build a tower that reached heaven,[19] while others believe that God was not angry but leveraged that event to accomplish His original instructions to Noah by sending the people out to populate the earth, purposefully creating different cultures.[20] Consider this: they never would have been able to create new languages on their own. This was a divine act of God.

Verse 8 tells us that God caused the people to move out and away from each other to populate the world. It's likely people who shared the same language settled with one another. Over time, they married within their groups, began families, and developed their own traditions and cultures. Our colorful, diverse world today reflects the outcome of that story so long ago.

Think about your life experiences. What are some positives you've discovered in meeting and interacting with people of other races and nationalities?

If you have limited experiences to draw from, can you speculate on the kinds of things you might be missing out on?

Knowing that God purposefully introduced different colors and cultures into the world should motivate us to embrace those who are different from us, remembering that our differences are desirable and good.

3. God condemns any action that undermines the gospel and the dignity of His creation, because He sent Jesus to die for everyone.

The purpose of today's lesson is to give us a glimpse into the heart of God when it comes to division within the body of Christ, especially as that division relates to our differences. Just as Paul elevated the gospel to the Galatians in hopes that they would guard their hearts against the deceptive words of the Judaizers, it's up to us to guard our hearts against beliefs or behaviors that would undermine the gospel by creating division between us and other believers.

One of the ongoing divisions within the church concerns our different colors and cultures, as well as the impact of racism as a barrier to unity. During a discussion after one of his speeches, Dr. Martin Luther King, Jr. told an audience that "...the church is still the most segregated major institution in America. At 11:00 on Sunday morning...we stand at the most segregated hour in this nation."[21]

There have been times in human history, including American church history, when the Bible was used to justify injustice against minority people groups. However, as believers who recognize that we are one in Christ, this is our opportunity to stand up and speak out.

In their book *Black and White: Disrupting Racism One Friendship at a Time*, church staffers Teesha Hadra and John Hambrick write about discovering a friendship as a black woman and white man. As they write about race and the gospel, they challenge believers with this observation: "People who call Jesus their Lord and Savior can no longer afford to merely engage in idle, albeit distressed conversation about racism. At best, the watching world reads our inaction as proof of our irrelevance. At worst, we give the world another reason to reject the gospel. The church cannot let that stand."[22]

Jesus said that the world will know we are His disciples by our love for one another (John 13:35)—by how we care for, defend, and protect others regardless of skin color or any other differences threatening to separate us or cause division. Yet, part of our struggle is that we don't always know what to do in response to racism and other injustices in our world.

When we don't know what to do, Scripture is always the first place we should turn. Here are some insights from Scripture about injustice and how we should respond to it:

Read PPhilippians 2:6-8. For whom are we to speak up?

Turn to Jeremiah 22:3, and list the actions we are instructed to take on behalf of those who are treated unjustly:

Micah 6:8 defines three things that God says are good for us to do. What are they?

As we reflect on these verses, two things are clear:

1. The Bible recognizes that injustice exists.
2. We should take action when we witness injustice against others.

In conversations I've had with women who've written me about race, grace, and the gospel, one of the common concerns shared is whether talking about different colors, cultures, or injustices is a spiritual issue or a social issue. Regardless of what we might call it, I believe it is an issue that God cares about deeply. Based on what we see in the Bible about God's character, we can be sure that He hates injustice. And so should we!

Look again at the actions you listed above. Are there any steps you need to take in order to speak up for those who don't have a voice or whose voice is not honored as it should be?

If so, for whom are you feeling called to advocate, represent, or defend? If not, what is holding you back?

As you consider what you've read and learned today, what are one or two takeaways that you want to remember?

Ah-ha Moment

Did you notice any ah-ha spiritual breakthrough moments in today's study, your prayer time, or your daily activities? If so, record that moment on the final page of this week's study (page 107).

There's so much more on this topic that I would like to share with you. I am encouraged by renewed interest in and conversation about unity in the body of Christ and racial reconciliation among believers. These discussions bring me hope that one day we can be the answer to Jesus's prayer for unity. As we live out the gospel in our lives each day, may we reflect God's heart for unity within our diversity.

Prayer

God, thank You for showing us how to honor our differences with one another. As I consider the world around me, help me to see and treat all people with the same love and value that You show them; in Jesus's name. Amen.

Weekly Breakthrough Reflection Exercise

Each day this week you have been prompted to record on this page any ah-ha spiritual breakthrough moments you've had in your study, prayer time, or daily activities. Take time now to reflect once more on where you've seen God working in your heart, mind, and life this week, and add any other ah-ha moments below.

Lightbulb
You gain new understanding about God or yourself.

Describe the moment:

_____

_____

_____

Butterfly
You surrender or let go of a struggle, sin, or stronghold from your past.

Describe the moment:

_____

_____

_____

Rainbow
You find new or renewed hope based on God's promises for your life.

Describe the moment:

_____

_____

_____

Busted Brick Wall
You confront and face up to any kind of fear or worry.

Describe the moment:

_____

_____

_____

Line in the Sand
You realize that a sin, struggle, or stronghold is no longer acceptable.

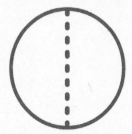

Describe the moment:

_____

_____

_____

Split-the-Rock
You have a supernatural shift in your faith or circumstances after faithfully praying and letting God lead.

Describe the moment:

_____

_____

_____

Choose one of your ah-ha moments from the previous page and describe it here:

What is a spiritual breakthrough you're still praying for?

Option: Write a prayer below:

Video Viewer Guide
WEEK 3

Scriptures: John 17:20-23, Galatians 3:28, 1 Corinthians 1:10, Acts 2:42-44,

Ephesians 4:2-6

The gospel _____.

The gospel _____.

The gospel _____.

Freedom Principle #3

Your freedom in Christ cannot be _____ or _____ away by someone who chooses not to live like Christ.

Finding Freedom

Memory Verse

Dear brothers and sisters, I plead with you to live
as I do in freedom from these things,
for I have become like you Gentiles—
free from those laws.
(Galatians 4:12)

Freedom Principle

Freedom in Christ is living free from fear
and fully alive with joy and purpose.

In Luke 15, Jesus tells the story of a young man who left home after asking his father for his share of the inheritance before his father died. The father agreed to his son's request, and the young man left home. Jesus tells about the son's escapades and how he spent all that his father had given him on what Jesus describes as wild living.

Then his—or rather, his daddy's—money ran out.

While Jesus tells this story to an audience, I've always wondered when the son might have realized that his money was about gone. Was it when he planned to show off that he could afford something extravagant but came up short? Did he discover his almost empty pockets right before he planned to buy an expensive trinket to impress a young lady?

The answer to that question doesn't matter, but it makes me think about the times in my own life when I thought I was in charge of my world and then discovered I didn't have enough. Times when I thought that my career had put me on top of the world only to be disappointed, or other times when my self-righteous pride came crashing down.

Such times are when people say, "Ah, that's when she hit rock bottom." Yet rock bottom doesn't necessarily equal repentance. From my own observations and life experience, I've seen plenty of people hit rock bottom and get really comfy there. Once or twice in life, I've been one of those people who realized that a habit or behavior wasn't healthy or helpful, but I wasn't ready to change.

Jesus continues the story by explaining that the destitute young man got a job feeding pigs, which would have been considered a deplorable position to Jesus's audience. Again, if I use some biblical imagination, I see that young man waking up day after day, passing by the places where he once partied on his way to feed the messy, smelly pigs. I'm pretty sure that as his body worked, his mind reflected on everything that had happened in his life.

That's when that young man experienced a breakthrough moment:

"When he came to his senses, he said, 'How many of my father's hired servants have food to spare, and here I am starving to death! I will set out and go back to my father and say to him: Father, I have sinned against heaven and against you. I am no longer worthy to be called your son; make me like one of your hired servants.'"

(Luke 15:17-19 NIV)

What made this a spiritual breakthrough? It was the moment when the young man realized that he could go back home. I don't know if that moment happened on his first day feeding pigs or the five-hundredth day. In my mind's eye, I see him sitting up straight with the realization that there was new hope in front of him.

So, the young man traveled home. He didn't expect much because anything that his dad would give him would be better than starving or feeding pigs.

What happened next is beautiful. It's also a precious illustration of the gospel of grace:

Extra Insight

Gospel: God became one of us to free us from the sin that was destroying us because we couldn't rescue ourselves.

"But the father said to his servants, 'Quick! Bring the best robe and put it on him. Put a ring on his finger and sandals on his feet.... For this son of mine was dead and is alive again; he was lost and is found.' So they began to celebrate."

(Luke 15:22, 24 NIV)

The young man returned home hoping to at least be a servant, but the father restored him to the status of a son, just as if he'd never left. This story illustrates the gospel because we're like the prodigal son. We abandon God and run our own way. At the point when we hit the wall, or hit rock bottom, we tend to beat ourselves up. But if we're humble and wise, we come to our senses and come home to God. He never stands with His hands on His hips; rather, God welcomes us with open arms. He rejoices over us and restores us. This is the gospel.

This week we will dig into Galatians 4, which is all about our status as sons or daughters—children of God.

Day 1: Keep Moving Forward!

Big Idea

Legalism is a step backward in our faith, not forward.

Last week we saw that at the end of Galatians 3, Paul opened up a vital dialogue about our standing as children of God. As you'll recall, the new covenant merges all believers into one body in Christ—which not only makes it possible for Jews and non-Jews to be a part of God's family but also puts us all on the same level with one another. This would have been considered a radical idea in Paul's time, and it is a sharp reminder for us today of our equality in Christ.

Today as we dig into Galatians 4, we will see that Paul uses the metaphor of slavery to describe how their "works of the law" or legalism resulted in bondage, not freedom in their faith. The same can be true of us. We tell ourselves that if we can just live up to whatever standard that we've set for ourselves, then we'll feel free—or at least feel better. But that's not the case. Our constant striving only leads to more stress and more striving, never bringing true freedom.

Slavery can be a complicated metaphor for us in light of our nation's history of slavery, including the use of the Bible by some Christians in the past to justify slavery. Yet, understanding the biblical context for slavery can keep us from either glossing over or being triggered by this metaphor so that we do not miss out on the richness of what Paul was teaching.

First, let's define the term. A slave is "one who is no longer free and has no rights."[1] In ancient times, slavery was common in empires such as Egypt, Greece, and Rome. Remember, Paul was a Roman citizen and a Jew, so his context was likely based on the slavery practices of ancient Rome and Israel. During those times, people could be enslaved for being a prisoner of war, the victim of piracy, unable to pay a debt, abandoned at birth,[2] or kidnapped as a slave from another area of the world, as well as other reasons. An interesting note, in ancient Rome, race had nothing to do with slavery.[3]

As far as what the Bible teaches on slavery, one source notes, "…the Bible contains no direct call to abolish slavery. But the implications of the gospel, especially the ethic of love, stand in opposition to slavery."[4] Check out the information below that highlights some of the specific guidelines in the Mosaic law regarding how the Israelites were to treat fellow Israelite slaves.

MOSAIC LAW GUIDELINES FOR THE TREATMENT OF ISRAELITE SLAVES

Slaves were not to be mistreated but treated as hired servants. (Leviticus 25:39)

Slaves were to be freed after six years. (Exodus 21:2)

During the Year of Jubilee, all slaves were to be released, no matter how long they had served. (Leviticus 25:54)

Slaves could buy their freedom, or someone could buy their freedom for them. (Leviticus 25:47-49)

In some cases, a person could choose to remain a slave; he or she would receive a mark in their ear to signify that choice. (Exodus 21:5-6)

With this background in mind, let's move forward.

Read Galatians 4:1-3. When it comes to awaiting an inheritance, why did Paul say that children aren't any better off than slaves?

At the beginning of Galatians 4, Paul is still talking about the relay hand off between the Abrahamic covenant to Mosaic law to the new covenant. Although we are heirs to God's promise to Abraham, there was a time when the law "guarded" God's people, babysitting them and keeping them in line,

Extra Insight

Slavery was an accepted practice in our own country until 1865 when it was abolished by the thirteenth amendment to the Constitution. Even today, we are dealing with the ongoing ramifications of slavery and racism in our country, as well as the tragic effects of domestic and worldwide human trafficking. Oh, the pain of living in a fallen world! Yet another reason we need the gospel.

so to speak, until Jesus came. Paul's comment that children are not much better off than slaves, even though they will own everything that their father had, is a way of expressing the condition of God's people in the long stretch between the Abrahamic covenant and the new covenant.

Reread Galatians 4:3. What two analogies does Paul use to describe our former spiritual state of being?

C_____ and S_____

As we learned last week, the law was part of the relay between God's covenant with Abraham and Jesus's coming. So, in Galatians 4:3, Paul describes our spiritual condition as that of children and slaves. Children need principles to be basic, and the law was a basic setup to prepare the Jewish people for the coming of Christ. Likewise, just as slaves are in bondage, the Jewish people put themselves in bondage to their legalism of the law.

This is where Paul poked at the Judaizers while teaching the Galatians. By adding circumcision as an additional requirement to the gospel, the Judaizers made it seem like taking that step was more spiritual than basic belief in Jesus. However, Paul taught the opposite, that faith in Christ alone is sufficient. The truth is that the law wasn't sophisticated spirituality; it was a simple, step-by-step attempt to appear more spiritual. After all, it can seem to be easier to follow steps than to fully surrender to grace, allowing the Holy Spirit to change us from the inside out.

The implications of this truth in my own struggle with legalism resulted in a breakthrough moment for me. My "busted brick wall" breakthrough moment occurred during a battle with anxiety. I feared that I was failing God because I was overwhelmed by a busy family and career. I beat myself up all of the time for not reading my Bible or praying enough. In desperation to stop feeling guilty, I decided to believe that those verses about God's love applied to me all of the time, not just when I performed. As that truth began to grow in me, I stopped feeling like I had to jump through my To-Do, Do-More, and Do-Better hoops. Freedom began to fill my lungs, instead of suffocating fear. As a result, I discovered that I wanted to pray more and that I felt more connected to God. It was a beautiful breakthrough moment!

In writing about the law versus the fulfillment of the law in Christ, one scholar made this observation:

For some fifteen centuries, Israel had been in kindergarten and grade school, learning their "spiritual ABCs," so that they would be ready when Christ would come. Then they would get the full revelation, for Jesus Christ is the "Alpha and the Omega" (Rev. 22:13); He encompasses *all* the alphabet of God's revelation to man. He is God's last Word (Heb. 1:1-3).[5]

In other words, the law prepared the Jewish people for Jesus's coming. But when Jesus was revealed, they had the invitation to let go of the law and grab hold of Jesus's free offer of grace and love, which was far better than the law.

Read and summarize the following verses to compare the ABCs of the law with what Jesus taught.

The ABCs of the law	Jesus's Teachings
Exodus 20:13	Matthew 5:21-22
_____	_____
Exodus 20:14	Matthew 5:28
_____	_____
Leviticus 19:18	Matthew 5:44
_____	_____

In each of these pairings, the Old Testament law dictated specific actions and consequences, whereas Jesus's teaching is about the condition of the heart. As we've learned, the law could govern behavior, but only the Holy Spirit can transform a heart (Romans 2:29).

As I've thought about the relay between the Abrahamic covenant, Mosaic law, and the new covenant, I've wondered why God took so long to send Jesus. Why didn't God shorten the span of centuries between the law and the new covenant, especially since the Israelites had proven they couldn't live up to the righteousness of the law?

Read Galatians 4:4. According to this verse, God sent Jesus at what point in time?

While God could have sent Jesus at various times in human history, Galatians 4:4 tells us that He chose "the right time." But why was it the right time? Here is a summary of four possible reasons:

1. "It was the right time theologically." Hundreds of prophecies had been given by this point, and the law had been around long enough to point people to Christ.
2. "It was the right time religiously." The world was inundated with empty pagan practices, so there was a spiritual hunger among not only the Jewish people, but all the people of the world, particularly in Rome.
3. "It was the right time culturally." The gospel could reach around the world more easily since the Greek language had become so common.
4. "It was the right time politically." Rome conquered much of the known world and built an infrastructure that allowed for broader travel.[6]

Since God is all-knowing, all-powerful, and always present, then we can trust that He knew exactly the right time when Jesus should be born in history, even if it doesn't make sense to us. Furthermore, when it was time for Jesus to come, He demonstrated the kind of attitude and relationship with God we are to have that reflects the heart of the gospel.

Read Philippians 2:5-8 below.

Underline what Jesus gave up when He came to earth. (v. 7)
Circle the position that Jesus assumed. (v. 7)

⁵ *You must have the same attitude that Christ Jesus had.*

⁶ *Though he was God,*
he did not think of equality with God
as something to cling to.
⁷ *Instead, he gave up his divine privileges;*
he took the humble position of a slave
and was born as a human being.
When he appeared in human form,
⁸ *he humbled himself in obedience to God*
and died a criminal's death on a cross.

As you think about your attitude toward whatever you're dealing with in your life, what aspect of Jesus's example of humble servanthood challenges or inspires you today?

Jesus became a slave so that we could gain our freedom. That's so powerful! Rather than coming to earth to make sure we were following the rules, Jesus came to make a way for us to have a relationship with God. There's no amount of legalism in the world that motivates a person to lay down his or her life for others. Only love can do that.

Prayer

God, it's stunning to me that Jesus became a slave so that I could be free. Thank You for Jesus's attitude of humility, surrender, and sacrifice on my behalf. Help me to see where I'm taking a step back into legalism so that I can run freely and fully toward the loving example of Christ; in Jesus's name. Amen.

Day 2: Children of God

Ah-ha Moment

Did you notice any ah-ha spiritual breakthrough moments in today's study, your prayer time, or your daily activities? If so, record that moment on the final page of this week's study (page 141).

Pastor and author David Platt and his wife adopted two children, one from China and another from Kazakhstan. Since their adopted children look different than their parents, the Platts are often asked if they have children of their own. It's a question that David hates being asked. He says, "I want to say, 'Come in real close. I have a secret: they're ours!'"[7]

In our study today, Paul will teach us about our adoption into the family of God and the privilege of being children of God. In God's eyes, it doesn't matter where we come from or what we've been through; when we say "yes" to the gospel, God proclaims that we are His! As I wrote this lesson, my heart burst with the prayer, "God, if all believers would *truly* live as your sons and daughters, our lives and our world would never be the same!"

Even if you came from the best family, being a part of your family pales in comparison to being God's child. And if you came from a dysfunctional or broken family, the good news is that the gospel gives you the family that you wish you had! As you'll learn today, your standing as not only an heir but also a child of God renews and restores beyond what you've lost or never have had in your earthly family. It's more than just possible. This is what God has promised.

Big Idea

As children of God, we all enjoy "son status"!

Read Galatians 4:5 (NLT) and complete the following:

God sent [Jesus] to buy _____ for us who were slaves to the law, so that he could _____ us as his very own _____.

The gospel message is that God became one of us to free us from the sin that was destroying us because we couldn't become righteous on our own. God didn't send Jesus to save us and then mistreat us. God adopted us as His very own children with all of the rights and privileges that come with being a part of His family.

How would you describe the difference between a child who is staying with a family in foster care and a child who is fully adopted into a family?

When I reflect on various ah-ha spiritual breakthroughs in my life—whether it was a lightbulb moment when I took a step toward trusting God more, or a busted brick wall moment when I confronted a fear—one benefit of those breakthroughs was that I felt closer to God and more like a member of His family. An indicator that I felt closer to God was a desire to be obedient not because of rules, but because I felt a connection with God. Another indicator was that I was able to tell God everything that was on my heart and mind without holding back. Once I truly settled into my standing as God's daughter, I felt secure in my relationship with God, which relaxed my fear-based need to keep following rules.

When do you feel a connection with God?

When do you feel unloved by God?

In the Old Testament, the Israelites couldn't approach God directly as we can today. In fact, there were dire consequences for drawing physically near to God. In Exodus 19:12, God told Moses to keep the Israelites away from Mount Sinai where Moses was receiving the law from God: "Anyone who touches the mountain will certainly be put to death." Additionally, only the high priest could enter the Holy of Holies once a year to make atonement for the sins of the people (Leviticus 16:34).[9]

But that changed when Jesus died on the cross and the curtain in the Temple was torn from top to bottom (Matthew 27:51). As we read in Hebrews 10:20, "Jesus opened a new and life-giving way through the curtain into the Most Holy Place." Now, not only can we draw near to God as children of God, our special relationship gives us the privilege of calling out to God in a special way.

According to Galatians 4:6, what can we call God?

This is huge! Our invitation to call God our *Abba* or daddy means that we can come near to God as children under the new covenant in Christ. Furthermore, one author explains that this invitation to call God *Abba* is more than a child sweetly saying the word *Daddy*; rather, it's more emotionally-driven, like "a groaning, a longing for a father."[10] I think that this interpretation resonates with us because we want a daddy who kisses and snuggles and we also *need* a daddy who is there for us in difficulty and distress. Just as a loving earthly father relates to his children in more than one way, God relates to us as *Abba* Father in many ways, too.

For some of us, connecting with God as Father is difficult because of a disappointing or hurtful experience with an earthly father. Here's a fact that every one of us must remember: Even the best earthly father cannot compare to God as Abba Father.

Read Hebrews 4:16 in the margin. When we come near to God, how will He respond?

Let us then approach God's throne of grace with confidence, so that we may receive mercy and find grace to help us in our time of need.

(Hebrews 4:16 NIV)

How are we to approach God?

I remember a difficult period in our family after conducting an addiction intervention that didn't go well. Devastated, I cried out to God in the prayer closet in my office each morning for weeks. During that time in my life, I was far too broken and burdened to think about fancy prayers or to bargain. All I could do was wrap myself in a blanket, sink onto the little stool in the closet, and cry out to God. Rules couldn't fix my family's situation. What I needed in that moment was a God who was present in my pain. In time, the knowledge of God's presence gave me the strength to ask for God's power to change *me*, something that I couldn't do on my own. My Abba Father knew me, and He knew what needed to be transformed within me. It was a work that I couldn't do on my own, but the Father did it within me. He exposed the pride, fear, impatience, and control issues that I'd masked with my recipe of spiritual activities.

Not only does the gospel make it possible for us to approach God as our Abba Father; it makes us the recipients of so much more.

Read Galatians 4:7 (NLT) and complete the following:

You are no longer a _____ *but God's own* _____. *And since you are his child, God has made you his* _____.

Depending on your family, inheritances come in all forms. In the Bible, whatever wealth that a family had was passed from the father to his sons. Usually, the oldest son received double the inheritance as any other brother in order to take care of his mother and sisters in the event of his father's death. Yet as one source explains, "To the Hebrew mind, the term 'inheritance' had strong spiritual and national associations extending far beyond the family estate."[11]

So, it's a big deal when Paul teaches that we're no longer slaves but God's sons (and daughters); we are His children. As one writer puts it, "For a child of God, there is a confidence and boldness every day. We don't walk in fear of anyone or anything; our Father owns the place."[12]

This also means that we're equal heirs to all that God has.

Have you ever inherited anything? If so, what did that inherited item mean to you?

Inheritances are gifts generally given after death. When we use the word *inheritance*, it usually means that something of value will be passed along. My grandmother didn't have much earthly wealth, but when she passed away, I

received something that I consider priceless to me: her perfume. Grandma's scent was as much a part of who she was as her smile and giant servant's heart. Even now, whenever I sniff her perfume, my mind instantly floods with all of my favorite memories of her love and presence in my life. It may not be worth a lot of money, but it helps me maintain a priceless connection with someone I loved, and who loved me so much.

As children of God, what is our inheritance?

Read 1 Peter 1:3-5 (NIV) below. Circle the phrases "great mercy," "new birth," and "living hope."

How do we receive our new birth and living hope?

How is our eternal inheritance described?

³ *Praise be to the God and Father of our Lord Jesus Christ! In his great mercy he has given us new birth into a living hope through the resurrection of Jesus Christ from the dead,* ⁴*and into an inheritance that can never perish, spoil or fade. This inheritance is kept in heaven for you,* ⁵*who through faith are shielded by God's power until the coming of the salvation that is ready to be revealed in the last time.*

Read 2 Peter 1:3-4 (NIV) below. Circle the phrase "great and precious promises." Underline what God gives to us by His divine power (v. 3).

³ *His divine power has given us everything we need for a godly life through our knowledge of him who called us by his own glory and goodness.* ⁴*Through these he has given us his very great and precious promises, so that through them you may participate in the divine nature, having escaped the corruption in the world caused by evil desires.*

According to verse 4, why does God give us these gifts?
So that . . .

All of us have become like
one who is unclean,
*   and all our righteous acts*
*   are like filthy rags;*
we all shrivel up like a leaf,
*   and like the wind our sins*
*   sweep us away.*

(Isaiah 64:6 NIV)

Have you ever watched the television show "Hoarders"? It portrays people who struggle with mental health issues such as anxiety or obsessive-compulsive disorder, often with underlying trauma issues. The result is an obsessive need to hold on to material possessions, even after the items have expired or have toxically degraded. The show documents the difficulties in treatment as well as the small triumphs along the way.

We might look at our legalistic efforts as a kind of spiritual hoarding. Here on earth we tend to be fixated on our To-Do, Do-More, and Do-Better hoops, hoping that our efforts are creating some kind of special spiritual wealth. Yet, God calls us to let go of our religious self-effort, because whatever we're holding on to isn't spiritual wealth, but rather "filthy rags" as described in Isaiah 64:6. God wants us to shift our attention to what is available to us right now!

Extra Insight

What part of our divine inheritance is available to us for daily use now?

Riches of His **grace**
Riches of His **glory**
Riches of His **goodness**
Riches of His **wisdom**[13]

Read Matthew 6:19-21 below. Draw one line under what you should not do, and draw two lines under what you should do.

[19] **"Don't store up treasures here on earth, where moths eat them and rust destroys them, and where thieves break in and steal.** [20] **Store your treasures in heaven, where moths and rust cannot destroy, and thieves do not break in and steal.** [21] **Wherever your treasure is, there the desires of your heart will also be."**

(Matthew 6:19-21)

What does it mean to store treasures in heaven?

How could your hoarding of spiritual To-Do, Do-More, and Do-Better behaviors get in the way of you experiencing the treasures that God has for you now?

How could those behaviors hinder you from storing treasures in heaven?

Even as we live in a world where wealth is desired, God wants to give you so much more! I pray that you live in the riches of God's grace, glory, goodness, and wisdom each and every day.

Prayer

Dear God, I want to live in the riches of what You provide for me as Your child. Thank You for the riches of Your grace, Your glory, Your goodness, and Your wisdom in my life.

Today, as I am trying to deal with _____ _____, *I come confidently to You, thanking You for the mercy and grace You've promised to give me. Help me to* _____ _____.

In Jesus's name. Amen.

Day 3: Knowing God Defines Who You Are

After twenty-five years of marriage, I became single again due to divorce. Perhaps you've been through a life experience where your identity also took a major shift, whether for good or bad:

Career change or ministry transition...
Major health diagnosis...
Job loss...
Marriage, divorce, widowhood...
Infertility...
Having/losing children...
Significant weight loss or gain...

When our identity changes, even if for good reasons, the process of reorienting ourselves can throw our thoughts, emotions, and actions into chaos. The question *Who am I?* can seem to drive everything we think and do.

Ah-ha Moment

Did you notice any ah-ha spiritual breakthrough moments in today's study, your prayer time, or your daily activities? If so, record that moment on the final page of this week's study (page 141).

Big Idea

When you know who you are in Christ, your confidence no longer hinges on what you do.

For me, I picture identity changes in my life like traveling through a long tunnel. In my part of the country, there's a long tunnel through a large mountain in Pennsylvania. When my car enters one end of the tunnel, it's impossible to see the opening at the other end. Sometimes the tunnel is dark and sometimes there is heavy traffic, and in either instance my focus is to stay in my lane and travel wisely, adjusting my speed according to what I can see clearly. But, I'm always looking out for the end of the tunnel. I never forget that it's there, even when I can't see it.

Some tunnels in our lives are short and some are long. I actually went through a dark tunnel of depression for a short period of time during my divorce because I struggled with the transition from identifying as "married" to "single." In the midst of that journey were a lot of dark days and difficult questions that I had to ask along the way. But God used this as a breakthrough experience in my life. By the way, even though I knew I'd come out the other side, that truth didn't diminish the darkness and difficulty of that journey.

As we continue studying Galatians 4 today, we'll learn from Paul's concern for the Galatians and their lack of understanding regarding their identity in Christ. They allowed themselves to be drawn by the Judaizers into a dark tunnel and back into To-Do and Do-More behaviors. While frustrated and a little discouraged, Paul continues to compel them to remember the power of the gospel in their lives.

Read Galatians 4:8-9. While the Israelites were slaves to the law, what were the Gentiles slaves to before they heard the gospel?

Before Paul arrived to preach the gospel, the Galatians worshipped pagan gods. When Paul and Barnabas traveled to Galatia to preach the gospel for the first time, they stopped in the city of Lystra and healed a man who had been lame from birth. Then the crowd found out that the man was miraculously healed. What happens next paints a picture of the Galatians' spiritual past as well as Paul's commitment to sharing the gospel, even when it almost cost him his life.

Read Acts 14:11-20. Whom did the crowd believe Paul and Barnabas to be?

Paul and Barnabas _____ their clothes in despair. (v. 14)

Summarize Paul and Barnabas's message to the crowd found in verses 15-18:

How did the crowd respond? (v. 18)

After the Jews showed up and riled up the crowd, they _____ Paul. (v. 19)

The Galatians lived in the midst of rampant paganism and idol worship. At one point the priest of Zeus brought out bulls to sacrifice to Paul and Barnabas (Acts 14:13). Imagine Paul standing in that situation as a man sent by God to share the gospel, and the people thought that he was a god, not one who served God. Rather than try to reason with the people, Paul and Barnabas elevated the gospel as their answer in the midst of that mess.

Then came the "are-you-kidding-me" moment when the Jews showed up. Instead of protecting Paul as a fellow Jew, they turned the crowd against him in a violent way. The crowd threw stones at Paul, which was attempted murder! While that story ended with Paul leaving town, eventually a church was planted in that city and people came to know Christ. Years later, the Galatians' pagan roots, which had caused them to try to please idols, regrew into legalism, which led them to try to please God.

It wasn't Paul's teaching or the gospel that failed; it was the Galatians' unwillingness to believe that the gospel was enough. One writer observes, "They were giving up the power of the gospel for the weakness of the law."[14]

Two questions that Paul posed to the Galatians are worth our consideration today.

Read Galatians 4:9 in the margin, and answer the two questions for yourself in the space below:

But now that you know God—or rather are known by God—how is it that you are turning back to those weak and miserable forces? Do you wish to be enslaved by them all over again?
(Galatians 4:9 NIV)

Paul's two questions in Galatians 4:9 challenged the Galatians to reflect on the gift of the gospel that they'd been given versus returning to the bondage of slavery. One writer says it like this: "If your Christianity consists of slavery to religion in order to make yourself right with God, then it's just as if you're giving yourself to the pagan religions of the world."[15] Paul implored the Galatians to realize that there was so much they would miss out on if they plunged back into legalism. The same goes for us!

The gospel makes it possible for us to know God in a personal way. It opens the door to our ability to pray boldly and confidently to God as well as experience the guidance of the Holy Spirit within us. Being known by God means we're a part of His family and our name is written in what the Bible calls the Book of Life (Revelation 3:5, Revelation 20:12), which records our names as believers and inheritors of eternal life.

Galatians 4:10 expands upon the questions in verse 9, acknowledging that Paul's audience was inclined to observe not only circumcision but also certain religious festivals and holidays. The law outlined a number of religious events, and it seems the Galatians may have used their preparation and participation in these events as a kind of To-Do, Do-More, and Do-Better legalism in order to win God's favor.

Does this mean we shouldn't celebrate holidays that have religious histories or meaning? Not at all! Rather, we should celebrate because of our freedom in Christ, not because we're hoping for God's favor because we showed up.

Read Galatians 4:11. What was Paul's concern for the Galatians?

The gospel message had not changed, no matter how many times Paul had repeated it and the Galatians had heard it. So, if it seems that Paul was exasperated and frustrated in verse 11, that's true. Remember what he had personally experienced in his own break from legalism, his gospel transformation, and his sacrifice to bring the gospel to the Galatians. After seeing so many of them accept Christ and then begin a church, it would be hard *not* to become discouraged when so many were following the self-righteous and misguided path of the Judaizers.

So, Paul pulled out some passion and pleading as he appealed to the wayward believers.

What was Paul's appeal to the people in Galatians 4:12?

Paul continued his pleas in Galatians 4:19-20. What was his hope for them?

Paul realized that the Galatians had to make a choice about how they were going to live. He couldn't do that for them. This is a powerful example for us, especially those of us who struggle with control issues.

There may be people in our lives who are making reckless and unwise decisions in their spiritual lives—such as skipping or avoiding church, being influenced by relationships with legalistic Christians, or reading and watching material that isn't aligned with the gospel. All of that can be difficult for us to observe. Although we can express our best hopes for them and encourage them toward the gospel, we're not in control of others.

Is there a situation in your life where you need to let go of trying to "fix" someone's faith?

The only person you and I can control is ourself. So, let's wrap up today by focusing on ourselves and coming back to the question, "What is my identity in Christ?" This is an important question that provides an unshakable foundation as we move through different ages and stages in our lives.

During my divorce, I talked with a friend about my struggle to adjust to my new identity. She asked me to pray and ask God to give me a "new name"—in other words, to ask God to guide me toward seeing myself in my new identity. While my status as a child of God had not changed, there was a big piece of me that had and I needed help refocusing.

I sat down with my journal and began to write and pray. Over the course of a few days, I felt God speaking into my heart about who I am in His eyes. Here's what I received one beautiful spring day. It was God's "new name" message to me in the form of an identity statement:

You are God's beautiful, valuable, capable daughter.
You are confident in Christ.
You are worthy of God's best.

As I thought about this statement of my identity, I realized that each part is reflected in either the character of God or a promise that God has made in Scripture. These words also reflect the gospel truth and my now-and-eternal status as a child of God.

I believe these words are true not only for me but for you, too. If you're willing, I'd like you to conclude your time today by reflecting on these words for *your* life.

Fill in the blank with your name and read each statement aloud:

_____ is God's beautiful, valuable, capable daughter.

_____ is confident in Christ.

_____ is worthy of God's best.

Did you find this identity statement easy or hard to believe for yourself? Why?

Ah-ha Moment

Did you notice any ah-ha spiritual breakthrough moments in today's study, your prayer time, or your daily activities? If so, record that moment on the final page of this week's study (page 141).

Is there anything else you'd like to add to your statement as part of your identity in Christ?

Prayer

God, I've been through a lot of changes—and am going through changes now. Yet, at every stage, the gospel is true and transformative in my life. God, I want to walk and live in freedom today as who You've created me to be; in Jesus's name. Amen.

Day 4: Who's Your Mama?

As we're well into the letter now, perhaps you've noticed Paul's thoroughness in teaching the gospel from several different angles. Many of his teaching points appear counter to the various arguments and accusations posed by the Judaizers. In today's study, we will see Paul use Abraham's life to demonstrate another picture of the relationship between the gospel and the law. In Paul's teaching, he uses Abraham and Sarah's decision to leverage human effort to secure what God had already promised. While you might be familiar with this story from the Old Testament, there are some rich gospel lessons that you can glean from Paul's teaching today.

Big Idea

Our bad decisions, baggage, and brokenness are never too big for God's power and presence to guide us toward a life-changing breakthrough.

Read Galatians 4:21-26.

How are Abraham's two wives described in verse 22?

What did each woman represent? (vv. 24-25)

When God made the covenant with Abraham, the man had only one wife. However, Abraham and his wife, Sarah (formerly Sarai), were past their child-bearing years, and this perplexed them because God had promised them a child. Remember, Abraham was present for the covenant (when God passed through the split animals). So, why did Abraham end up with a free wife and a slave wife and one son from each? You don't have to know much about the Bible to know that this is a difficult situation.

Read Genesis 16:1-6 and mark the following T (true) or F (false).

___ 1. Abraham and Sarah had six children. (v. 1)

___ 2. Sarah's Egyptian slave was named Hagar. (v. 1)

___ 3. Sarah blamed God for her childless state. (v. 2)

___ 4. Abraham offered to marry Hagar and start a family. (v. 2)

___ 5. Hagar wasn't able to get pregnant after marrying Abraham. (v. 3)

___ 6. After Hagar got pregnant, she began to hate Sarah. (v. 4)

_____ **7. Sarah began to blame Abraham for the tension between her and Hagar. (v. 5)**

_____ **8. Sarah tried to be nicer to Hagar, and their relationship improved. (v. 6)**

Wasn't this the same Abraham who believed God's promise and whose faith was counted by God as righteousness? Yes. It seemed he developed a case of what I like to call *flaky faith*, which is a palatable way of saying that while Abraham may not have doubted the truth of God's promise, he definitely doubted God's plan and timeline. When I reflected on Abraham and Sarah's situation in my *I'm Waiting, God* Bible study, I offered this conclusion: "Impatience does result in a baby—and a lot of bitter feelings, too."[16]

What went down between Abraham, Sarah, and Hagar wasn't good for many reasons. It's tempting to give their situation some of the side-eye that we generally reserve for reality television stars who make bad decisions, but have you ever tried to "help God out" and wound up in a big mess?

While Paul uses Sarah and Hagar as an illustration for the Galatians, there is an underlying theme that I don't want us to miss: Our bad decisions, baggage, or brokenness are never too big for God's power and presence to guide us toward a life-changing breakthrough.

Read Genesis 16:15. What did Hagar name her son?

Now read Genesis 21:2-3. What name did Abraham give Sarah's son?

Thirteen years passed between the births of Ishmael and Isaac. Take a moment and imagine what it would have been like to live in the home with Abraham, Sarah, Hagar, and the two boys—teenage Ishmael and infant Isaac. Not only was Abraham dealing with two wives and two sons with a wide age gap between them, but I wonder if he also carried the weight of knowing that he didn't wait for God's timing.

Now think about what it must have been like for Ishmael, specifically. When his mother, Hagar, was pregnant, an angel of the LORD had told her that he would be "a wild donkey of a man" and in conflict against everyone (Genesis 16:12). Just imagine that temperament in the teen years!

Read Genesis 21:9. What was Ishmael doing during the family feast?

Genesis 21 reveals the beginnings of that prophetic word as Ishmael mocks Isaac, making fun of the toddler boy. While the Scripture doesn't give any insight into this, I wonder if he might have overheard Sarah and Abraham discussing that he wasn't the child God promised but a human plan that turned into a pain for everyone.

Paul uses Ishmael's treatment of Isaac as a teaching illustration for the Galatians.

Read Galatians 4:28-29, and complete the following with either Isaac or Ishmael:

Believers in Christ are children of the promise like

_____.

Those who want to keep the law are like _____.

Ishmael illustrates the law of human effort because, by arranging for his conception, Abraham and Sarah were trying to get something that God had already promised to give them. Isaac represents the power of the Spirit, though God's supernatural intervention was needed for Sarah to conceive and bear a child at her age.

For each pair of words below, write S (Sarah) or H (Hagar) in the blank to match each woman with what she represents. (Refer back to Galatians 4:21-26 if needed.)

Sarah = S   Hagar = H

_____ 1. Freeborn wife

_____ 2. Slave wife

_____ 3. Mt. Sinai (law)

_____ 4. The Jerusalem
           above (freedom)

_____ 5. God's promise

_____ 6. Human effort

_____ 7. Isaac (born by the
           power of the Spirit)

_____ 8. Ishmael (born
           according to the flesh)

In the final verses of Galatians 4, Paul returns to the metaphor of slavery to wrap up his contrast of the two covenants using Hagar and Sarah.

Read Galatians 4:30-31. Who will not share in the inheritance of the free woman's son?

It may seem pretty harsh that Paul would say someone isn't worthy of God's inheritance. But remember, Paul is using Hagar's status as a slave as a metaphor for legalistic behavior, which does not trust that believing God is enough. However, as a human being, Hagar was *not* forgotten by God. Let's take a look at how Hagar and Ishmael's story concluded.

Look up Genesis 21 and answer the following questions:

When Abraham voiced his concerns about Ishmael, what did God tell him about Ishmael's future (even though we know from Genesis 16:12 that Ishmael would be a difficult person to be around)? (v. 12)

Why did Hagar put Ishmael under a bush when their food and water ran out? (v. 16)

What message did God speak to Hagar about her son? (v. 17)

How do verses 20-21 summarize Ishmael's life?

When I reflect on Hagar's story, three takeaways stand out to me.

1. **Hagar was freed from slavery.** Though Sarah treated Hagar badly during her pregnancy and Abraham sent Hagar and Ishmael away, the ultimate outcome for Hagar—being freed from slavery—was a good thing.

2. **God did not abandon Hagar in her wilderness.** My heart breaks each time I read the part where Hagar put Ishmael under a bush and walked away so that she wouldn't see him die. By this point, Ishmael was a teen boy, so she may have had to carry him because he'd lost his strength. Yet, God showed up, spoke words of encouragement, and sent help when they needed it most. As Paul talks about how Ishmael is the symbol of slavery and the law, I'm reminded that God still shows up in the lives of those who cling to legalism. Who we are does not stop God from being faithful to who He is.

3. **Hagar and Ishmael found a new home and future.** I love the words of Genesis 21:20, "God was with the boy as he grew up" (NIV). Even though Ishmael wasn't given son status, he was not abandoned by God. In fact, God being with him means that Ishmael's life mattered, even if it began through an act of fear and lack of trust.

> **What are some of *your* takeaways from the story of Abraham, Sarah, and Hagar?**

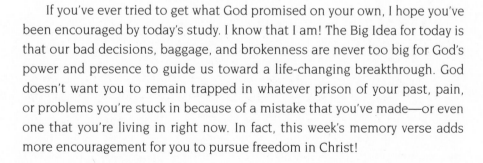

If you've ever tried to get what God promised on your own, I hope you've been encouraged by today's study. I know that I am! The Big Idea for today is that our bad decisions, baggage, and brokenness are never too big for God's power and presence to guide us toward a life-changing breakthrough. God doesn't want you to remain trapped in whatever prison of your past, pain, or problems you're stuck in because of a mistake that you've made—or even one that you're living in right now. In fact, this week's memory verse adds more encouragement for you to pursue freedom in Christ!

Memory Verse Reflection

> **This week's memory verse is Galatians 4:12. Write it on the following page, putting your name in the space provided.**

Ah-ha Moment

Did you notice any ah-ha spiritual breakthrough moments in today's study, your prayer time, or your daily activities? If so, record that moment on the final page of this week's study (page 141).

Big Idea

With practice, you can create space for breakthrough moments to occur.

Dear _____,

I plead with you to _____

_____

_____.

(Galatians 4:12 NLT)

Tomorrow's study is an extended Breakthrough Reflection Exercise with a guided prayer I've written to give you an opportunity to strip away anything that has slowed you down or left you stalled or stuck in your faith or life. Tomorrow's lesson will take the same amount of time as usual, but it would be helpful for you to arrange to work through the content in a quiet space so that you can think and reflect.

Prayer

Dear God, thank You for the examples of the lives of Abraham, Sarah, and Hagar. While their story doesn't always reflect good decisions, I am grateful for Your faithfulness in my life and theirs. I am so glad that I am a child of Your promises, and I will walk in freedom today and not let anyone shake up the freedom that I have in You; in Jesus's name. Amen.

Day 5: Creating Room for Breakthrough

One of the most fascinating movie scenes for me is in the movie *The Shawshank Redemption*. The movie's main character, Andy Dufrene, is shown through flashbacks as he is making his way to freedom. That journey had begun one day when Andy, who was wrongly convicted of murder, discovered some loose cement on his cell block wall. Then for twenty long years, he dug his way to freedom one scoop at a time, slowly breaking through the crumbling cell block. On the night of his prison break, Andy escaped through his tunnel and then made a dramatic crawl through the prison's long, smelly septic pipe before he tumbled into a retaining pond outside the prison walls. That scene captures Andy standing up in the water in the darkness with the lightning illuminating his upraised hands and the raindrops falling on his relieved face.

At the beginning of our study, I explained that we can't force or plan breakthrough moments, but we can keep showing up faithfully one day at a time, letting God guide us and trusting that He will lead us to our breakthrough moments.

I've experienced quite a few breakthrough moments in my life in many different ways. The Weekly Breakthrough Reflection Exercise at the end of each week's lessons captures the kinds of breakthrough moments that I've experienced, and I hope you've been able to identify similar moments in your life as well. Again, breakthrough moments do not have to be as big as fireworks; rather, they can be revelations of all types that make you aware of where God is moving in your life.

The verses that inspire today's study are from another of Paul's letters:

> [1]*Therefore, I urge you, brothers and sisters, in view of God's mercy, to offer your bodies as a living sacrifice, holy and pleasing to God—this is your true and proper worship.* [2]*Do not conform to the pattern of this world, but be transformed by the renewing of your mind. Then you will be able to test and approve what God's will is—his good, pleasing and perfect will.*
>
> (Romans 12:1-2 NIV)

There are two practices in my life that help me to implement Romans 12:1-2, facilitating an atmosphere for breakthrough moments to occur. It's not that I expect breakthrough moments to happen each time I engage in these practices. They simply create space for breakthrough moments to occur. Here they are:

1. Weekly Shutdown (Sabbath)
2. Walking and Talking

Let's explore these practices together now, and it is my hope that you will try both of them over the next several days.

1. Weekly Shutdown Practice (Sabbath)

It's hard to offer our bodies as a living sacrifice to God (Romans 12:1) when our schedules are constantly jammed packed. For years, our society has complained that life is moving too fast. However, long ago God created a remedy to help us regulate the speed of our lives so that we don't overrun our capacity.

²By the seventh day God had finished the work he had been doing; so on the seventh day he rested from all his work. ³ Then God blessed the seventh day and made it holy, because on it he rested from all the work of creating that he had done.

(Genesis 2:2-3 NIV)

Then [Jesus] said to them, "The Sabbath was made for man, not man for the Sabbath."

(Mark 2:27 NIV)

Read Genesis 2:2-3 in the margin.

What did God do on the seventh day? What did He declare about this day?

Read Mark 2:27 in the margin. What did Jesus mean by this?

As part of the law, the Israelites were instructed to take one day a week to rest. This would have been such a radical cultural change for them. As former slaves in Egypt, they were used to working under brutal conditions all of the time. Not only did God want them to develop a rhythm of rest for their physical renewal, but God also knew that their minds needed rest and renewal as well.

When our minds are constantly in motion, filled with To-Do, Do-More, and Do-Better actions, we're not leaving God much room to speak into and adjust our thoughts, attitudes, or beliefs. Now, one of the reasons that we have To-Do, Do-More, and Do-Better impulses to begin with is because we believe that the more we do for God, the less fear or guilt we'll have that we're disappointing Him. So, one of the reasons God set apart one day as holy for worship and rest is so that we would have space, a gap, for Him to remind us of His love, presence, and provision.

Take a moment for a self-check related to both your physical and mental busyness.

On a scale of 1-10, how busy or active are you physically on a regular basis?

1	2	3	4	5	6	7	8	9	10
Inactive				Moderately Active				Constantly Active	

On a scale of 1-10, how busy is your mind on a regular basis?

1	2	3	4	5	6	7	8	9	10
It's real quiet				Steady				Overthinking	

When you are physically tired, how does that affect your emotional, mental, and spiritual well-being?

When you are mentally tired, how does that impact your physical, emotional, and spiritual well-being?

I've discovered that when I shut down my schedule for the day and engage in Sabbath rest, my mind gets to rest as much as my body. And when my mind and body are at rest, that is when God is at work renewing, realigning, and restoring what I cannot on my own.

TRY THIS: *Shutdown Day*

Look at your calendar and choose a day in the next week for a shutdown day. This day should be free from appointments or obligations. Your goal for the day is to practice being a child of God who trusts Abba Father to fill in the gaps for whatever problems you choose not to think through or actively solve.

For those who are thinking about the practical aspects of life, here are some guidelines for you, as well as some reflection questions you may use afterward.

Helpful Guidelines for a Shutdown Day

1. Avoid appointments or obligations.
2. Plan a crockpot meal, get take-out, or eat leftovers.
3. Turn off your electronic devices (at least for a period of time) to minimize distractions.
4. Lean into your family/friend relationships without pressure to accomplish anything.
5. After reflection, engage in activities that uplift you (for example, hobbies).

Shutdown Day Reflection Questions

After you try your first shutdown day, reflect on the following questions (you may want to record your responses in a notebook or journal).

1. How did it feel to focus on "being" and not "doing"? What did you do to rest physically and mentally?
2. How hard or easy was it for you to stop thinking of your To-Do, Do-More, or Do-Better lists? What helped you to let go?
3. How hard or easy was it to connect with God and rest in His presence? What helped you to experience God?
4. What did you pray about? How did you pray?
5. Did you sense God leading you to any insights about your needs or any spiritual breakthrough moments?

2. Walking and Talking Practice

But Jesus often withdrew to lonely places and prayed.
(Luke 5:16 NIV)

While Jesus didn't need a spiritual breakthrough, He did need a break from the constant noise and needs of people—including His own disciples. So, the idea of a walking and talking practice is inspired by Jesus.

Read Luke 5:16 in the margin. What did Jesus do on a regular basis?

"And you must love the Lord your God with all your heart, all your soul, all your mind, and all your strength."
(Mark 12:30)

Jesus went off alone to pray often. Most of the time, we emphasize Jesus going away to pray, which is a good thing. However, I'm reminded that for Jesus to get away, he had to walk. His two feet had to get into motion and propel Him away. It's not hard to imagine that while Jesus was walking, He swung his arms and, depending on how far he had to go, He might have broken out into a light sweat. As Jesus walked, it's likely that he prayed along the way.

If you are overwhelmed or stressed, be like Jesus and take regular walks. Medical researchers report that walking as exercise "behaves like medicine to improve brain health and thinking skills."[17]

In some translations of the Bible, the phrase "walked with God" is associated with people like Enoch (Genesis 5:24) and Noah (Genesis 6:9) whose hearts were faithful to God. We can imitate this metaphor by using walking and talking as a method to get away from the hustle and busyness of life to solely focus on God.

Read Mark 12:30 in the margin. What are the ways Jesus instructs us to love God?

We are more than just body; we are also spirit and soul (1 Thessalonians 5:23). God created our minds, hearts, souls, and bodies to work *interdependently*—as one. In other words, what affects one aspect of us affects all of us.

I walk and pray most days of the week. As I walk and pray, there's something about being outside in the natural world that God created that speaks to my soul. The activity of walking invigorates my physical self. And the fact that I'm not pursuing another agenda while I'm walking leaves space for the Holy Spirit to work within me.

I've experienced some of the most surprising spiritual, personal, and professional (related to my writing) breakthroughs while I'm walking. More than once, I've had to rush home to write everything down.

TRY THIS – *Walking and Talking* Exercise

Put on your shoes and take a walk. It doesn't matter if you walk inside on your treadmill or hike in the mountains. Unless you're planning to listen to worship music, leave your devices behind. Walk for fifteen minutes if you're trying this out for the first time. As you walk, you might begin talking with God by praying your favorite Bible verse. Here's an example:

> *Dear God, I know that Philippians 4:6-7 tells me to not be anxious about anything but to pray about everything. So today I am praying about _____. I believe that You know all about the situation and I can trust You to take care of it. Thank you for Your faithfulness in my life. I will walk in Your peace that passes all understanding; in Jesus's name. Amen.*

The goal of walking and talking is to allow your body to work while your mind connects with God and "relaxes." (P.S. If you're a regular walker or runner and you're already in the practice of walking/running and talking with God, then focus on the Shutdown Day practice.)

Walking and Talking Reflection Questions

After walking and talking, reflect on the following questions (you may want to record your responses in a notebook or journal).

1. How did it feel to combine walking and prayer?
2. Did you notice anything different about just walking without any agenda other than to connect with God?
3. What did you pray about?

Ah-ha Moment

Did you notice any ah-ha spiritual breakthrough moments in today's study, your prayer time, or your daily activities? If so, record that moment on the final page of this week's study (page 141).

4. Did you sense God leading you to any insights about your needs or any spiritual breakthrough moments?

Prayer

God, thank You for all the ways You've created me to connect with You. Help me to find the practices that facilitate my ability to just "be" with You rather than feel like I've always got to hustle. I am enough because of Your great love for me, expressed perfectly in what Jesus did for me. Thank You for that; in Jesus's name. Amen.

Weekly Breakthrough Reflection Exercise

Each day this week you have been prompted to record on this page any ah-ha spiritual breakthrough moments you've had in your study, prayer time, or daily activities. Take time now to reflect once more on where you've seen God working in your heart, mind, and life this week, and add any other ah-ha moments below. (You can experience more than one breakthrough in a particular category.)

Lightbulb
You gain new understanding about God or yourself.

Describe the moment:

_____

_____

_____

Butterfly
You surrender or let go of a struggle, sin, or stronghold from your past.

Describe the moment:

_____

_____

_____

Rainbow
You find new or renewed hope based on God's promises for your life.

Describe the moment:

_____

_____

_____

Busted Brick Wall
You confront and face up to any kind of fear or worry.

Describe the moment:

_____

_____

_____

Line in the Sand
You realize that a sin, struggle, or stronghold is no longer acceptable.

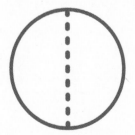

Describe the moment:

_____

_____

_____

Split-the-Rock
You have a supernatural shift in your faith or circumstances after faithfully praying and letting God lead.

Describe the moment:

_____

_____

_____

Choose one of your ah-ha moments from the previous page and describe it here:

What is a spiritual breakthrough you're still praying for?

Option: Write a prayer below:

Video Viewer Guide
WEEK 4

Scriptures: Galatians 4:6-7, Galatians 4:12, Galatians 21:20

Freedom means that we've been _____ and _____ to God.

The more _____ you follow, the less _____ you are.

Our bad decisions, baggage, or brokenness are never too big for God's _____ and _____ to guide us toward a life-changing breakthrough.

Freedom Principle #4

Freedom in Christ is living free from _____ and fully alive with joy and purpose.

Live Free!

Memory Verse

It is for freedom that Christ has set us free.
Stand firm, then, and do not let yourselves
be burdened again by a yoke of slavery.
(Galatians 5:1 NIV)

Freedom Principle

Spiritual breakthrough is
an ah-ha moment when we recognize
that God is at work within us, receive
what He's doing, and respond to it.

There are many people, events, and images in the Old Testament that serve as symbols or types of Jesus and the gospel message of the New Testament. Moses and the Israelites' exodus from Egypt are two of those symbols. First, Moses was born into slavery but raised by Pharaoh's royal family. Similarly, Jesus left royalty in heaven to become a slave for us (Philippians 2:6-8). Next, just as the Israelites were freed from over four hundred years of slavery when God sent Moses to Pharaoh, so we were freed from spiritual slavery when God sent Jesus to die for us.

For me, another symbolic illustration is found in Exodus 13. After the Passover when the Egyptians lost their firstborn sons for not letting God's people go, Pharaoh commanded the Israelites to leave. God's people were already prepared to get moving, so they hustled out of town toward the Red Sea.

However, Pharaoh changed his mind and sent his army after the Israelites to bring them back into slavery. Picture what it would be like to be an Israelite, finally free after a lifetime of oppression; just as you are on the cusp of owning your own skin again, you hear pounding hooves and see dust rising behind you as Pharaoh's soldiers, horses, and chariots charge your way. You're afraid not only of being captured but also of being taken captive and oppressed once again after being so close to living in freedom. Then, an obstacle to freedom looms so large and wide that your heart sinks to the bottom of your chest: the Red Sea in front of you. There are no boats to board for escape. You are trapped between an army and a wet grave.

As you read the following passage of Scripture, do so through the lens of everything you've learned so far about the gospel of grace and God's covenant with Abraham:

> [13] Moses answered the people, "Do not be afraid. Stand firm and you will see the deliverance the LORD will bring you today. The Egyptians you see today you will never see again. [14] The LORD will fight for you; you need only to be still."

> [29] But the Israelites went through the sea on dry ground, with a wall of water on their right and on their left. [30] That day the LORD saved Israel from the hands of the Egyptians, and Israel saw the Egyptians lying dead on the shore. [31] And when the Israelites saw the mighty hand of the LORD displayed against the Egyptians, the people feared the LORD and put their trust in him and in Moses his servant.

> (Exodus 14:13-14, 29-31 NIV)

This Old Testament story is a beautiful metaphor for the gospel. Not only did God free the Israelites from slavery; He rescued them from hopelessness and even death so that they could have a new life that brought new hope. But, as you know from learning about the law, those Israelites had a lot to learn about knowing and trusting God.

In this week's study, Paul calls the Galatian believers not only to know that they are free, but also to live as people who are free—to experience the freedom that Jesus promised.

Day 1: Stay Free

For years, I struggled with emotional eating. On the outside, I looked like a woman of normal body size. But inside a war raged between wanting to push down my stress with comfort food and letting go and trusting God. Food was a difficult temptation to manage. Permanent abstinence wasn't an option. I thought that I could free myself from that struggle with well-defined food plans. I put my faith in my measuring cups. I believed that if I could measure right-portioned amounts, then my emotional eating impulses could be controlled.

Oh, I was so wrong. I could pre-plan and pre-measure all I wanted, but still I longed for bowls of ice cream, French fries, and chocolate peanut brownies.

Years ago, a line-in-the-sand breakthrough moment came after I'd been praying for a few weeks about an emerging family crisis that was likely to drastically change our family. I told God that I was afraid I would eat my way right through it. And then I heard God's voice.

You don't need rules, Barb, you need Me.

I felt God leading me to surrender food one day a week in order to concentrate wholly on Him. Rather than try to control my struggle with To-Do, Do-More, and Do-Better lists, I prayed instead. As God sustained me through His word (Matthew 4:4), I discovered the deep satisfaction and freedom that I needed.

It's been five years since I began that weekly practice. On the annual anniversary of beginning my fast, I pray and ask God if I should stop or keep going. Fasting isn't a To-Do behavior to gain favor from God. It's a spiritual practice that creates space for God to give to me.

Is there a place of spiritual slavery in your life where you've tried to apply rules in order to maintain control rather than allow your relationship with God to lead you to freedom? If so, describe it briefly:

Write Galatians 5:1 below:

Before Paul wrote these words to the Galatians, Jesus gave the same message. Look up John 8:36 and write it below:

Look again at Galatians 5:1 above. What does Paul call us to do?

While the gospel is what God has done to set us free, Paul calls us to remain free by standing firm. In other letters written to different churches, Paul appeals to those believers to stand firm as well (1 Corinthians 16:13 and Philippians 4:1). Standing firm isn't about holding on to our justification (right standing) or our salvation in Christ. Rather, it aligns with sanctification, which is the process of becoming like Christ. We stand firm when we cooperate with what God is doing in our lives through intentionality and focus, making sure to guard against false messages and messengers.

What does standing firm look like for you? How do you stay intentional in what you listen to, read, or allow to influence your faith?

In the second week of our study, we discussed how justification is being made right with God when we receive salvation through faith in Christ. Justification is an act of God, not anything that we can do for ourselves. After justification, that's when God begins the ongoing process of *sanctification* within us. There are lots of fancy definitions for *sanctification*—which as we've said, is essentially being made into the likeness of Christ—but I appreciate the simplicity of Gehard Forde's definition: "Sanctification is . . . simply *the art of getting used to justification.*"[1]

Sanctification is a good thing! Imagine if God saved and justified us and then left us to flip and flop about every day with no hope of being able to handle the anxiety, impulses, shame, or anything else that can keep us stalled in a cycle of sin. While some people have experienced supernatural deliverance from certain sins, most of us still wrestle with selfish and sinful desires that can get out of control even though we love Jesus. Yet, God does not leave us on our own, but instead helps us to live according to our right standing with God—to become more and more like Jesus.

Here's a chart that shows the differences between justification and sanctification:

Justification	Sanctification
Legal standing (at salvation)	Internal condition
Once for all time	Continuous throughout life
Entirely God's work	We cooperate
Perfect in this life	Not perfect in this life
The same in all Christians	Greater in some than in others.[2]

Extra Insight

"Sanctification is a progressive work of God and [people] that makes us more and more free from sin and like Christ in our actual lives."[3]

The beauty of grace in both justification and sanctification is that *God works in us* without holding us responsible for the eternal impact of our sin. Remember, we're given status as children of God even though we don't deserve it.

Let's review. Write a definition for each term using your own words:

Justification is _____

Sanctification is _____

Justification is the process by which God transforms our standing or identity, and sanctification is the process by which God transforms our hearts and minds to look, sound, and think more like Christ. So, when you do your Bible study lesson, it's not the study itself that changes you, but how you allow God to use what you're studying to change you. When you pray, it's not what or when you pray that changes you, but how you allow God to transform your mind and heart as you pray.

Rules cannot "fix" us or free us; instead, we experience transformation and freedom as we live by faith.

Look at Galatians 5:1 again. Why doesn't Paul want believers to get tied up in slavery to the law?

Let your mind meditate on the first few words of Galatians 5:1. The New International Version says: "It is for freedom that Christ has set us free." Those words make me want to shout! Jesus didn't come to set us free because He wanted to shackle us or enslave us to His agenda. That wouldn't be freedom. He came to set us free so that we could stay free.

When Paul implores believers to avoid getting tied up again into slavery, he is echoing the teachings of Jesus, who accused the religious leaders in His time of dropping a heavy burden on God's people.

Read Matthew 23:2-4 in the margin. What was Jesus's specific criticism of the Pharisees and teachers of the law?

Now read Matthew 11:28-30 in the margin. What did Jesus say about His yoke?

Knowing what you know about the law and the gospel, why is Jesus's yoke better than the yoke of following religious rules?

Yokes fit over the necks of livestock, and in the Bible, a yoke "is a symbol of the burden or oppression of heavy responsibility, duty."[4]

The religious leaders and law-abiding Pharisees loved to use the law as a yoke to weigh down and discourage God's people. There were strict punishments for breaking the law, and the religious leaders handed out those punishments without grace or mercy. Remember, the point of the law was to help people understand God's holiness and see their sinfulness. However, the religious leaders used the law to puff themselves up with pride in their own self-righteousness.

Read Galatians 5:2-4. What is Paul's warning to those who are tempted to be circumcised?

As John Calvin once said, "Whoever wants half of Christ loses the whole."[5] Paul teaches the Galatians—and us—that we can't have both the law and the gospel. The gospel stops being the gospel if one drop of the law comes in.

[2] "The teachers of the law and the Pharisees sit in Moses' seat. [3] So you must be careful to do everything they tell you. But do not do what they do, for they do not practice what they preach. [4] They tie up heavy, cumbersome loads and put them on other people's shoulders, but they themselves are not willing to lift a finger to move them."
(Matthew 23:2-4 NIV)

[28] "Come to me, all you who are weary and burdened, and I will give you rest. [29] Take my yoke upon you and learn from me, for I am gentle and humble in heart, and you will find rest for your souls. [30] For my yoke is easy and my burden is light."
(Matthew 11:28-30 NIV)

Ah-ha Moment

Did you notice any ah-ha spiritual breakthrough moments in today's study, your prayer time, or your daily activities? If so, record that moment on the final page of this week's study (page 171).

Prayer

God, thank You for sending Jesus to set me free. I love that You want me to be free to enjoy freedom; You didn't set me free only to yoke me with a new set of rules. God, I hate that I still struggle with _____

_____ *, but like Paul, I believe that Your grace is sufficient for me (2 Corinthians 12:9). I want to cooperate with however You are working within me; in Jesus's name. Amen.*

Day 2: Obeying the Law Versus License to Love

Big Idea

Without all of the rules, we have lots of room to love!

When I was eight years old, my mom told me about Jesus dying on the cross for my sins. She shared the gospel with me after a series of sleepless nights and nightmares following a traumatic church movie night. How could a church movie night be traumatic? Well, a few decades ago, long before Jerry Jenkin's well-known "Left Behind" series came on the scene, a series of apocalypse movies were released. My little kid mind didn't understand everything that happened in the movies and how it related to the Bible; all I knew was this: I definitely didn't want to be left on the earth during the end time.

After mom explained the gospel to me, I prayed right there to ask Jesus into my heart. Whew. Relief. Or so I thought.

For the rest of my childhood and teen years, I experienced a lot of anxiety related to my faith. It wasn't something that I talked about, but the inner tumult brewed hot every day. I was so grateful that Jesus died for me and that I wouldn't be "left behind," but I lived with anxious fear that if I wasn't a perfect Christian, then maybe Jesus would change his mind about me.

In my book *Winning the Worry Battle*, I wrote this about my constant anxiety:

I grew up with a "look good on the outside" mind-set. I took pride in the fact that I was a good Christian kid. I didn't get in trouble.... But my heart suffocated under the burden of rules to keep me looking good on the outside. I struggled with myself on the inside and even worse, I judged people who struggle on the outside.[6]

What was the greatest tragedy of my struggle? It wasn't that I suffered from religious anxiety or that I felt suffocated under rules. The real bummer is that I missed out on what could have been a rich relationship with God and others.

Today our lesson is about the real reason you and I need to cut ties with legalism once and for all.

Turn to Galatians 5 and put a marker there. Read Galatians 5:9-10, and answer the following questions:

What analogy does Paul use to illustrate the rampant influence of false teaching?

What does Paul say will happen to those who confuse others with false teachings?

Using the analogy of yeast in verse 9, Paul illustrates how one lie can have such a devastating influence. So, Paul prophecies a judgment. Depending on your religious or church background, Paul's words of judgment on false teachers may bring a measure of comfort to you, especially if you experienced the Legalism Wheel rolling over you.

Now, in the next two verses, Paul brings the fire once more. In my opinion, this is his boldest statement yet to the Galatians.

Read Galatians 5:11-12. What does Paul want the false teachers to do to themselves?

Paul is being real with his feelings right here, but he's not being vengeful toward the troublemakers; rather, he's expressing how upset he is by how their false teachings have derailed the Galatian believers.

The next section of Paul's teaching is an ongoing source of challenge as well as breakthrough moments for me. We're going to spend the rest of today's study talking about how love—more specifically, how our freedom in Christ—gives us abundant reasons and opportunities to love God and others.

Extra Insight

"If you love people (because you love Christ), you will not steal from them, lie about them, envy them, or try in any way to hurt them. Love in the heart is God's substitute for laws and threats."[7]

Read Galatians 5:13, and answer the following questions.

Freedom should not be used to satisfy _____

_____.

Freedom should be used to _____

_____ **in love.**

To address the Judaizers' assumption that the "easy believism" of the gospel would lead to an anything-goes mindset among the Galatian believers, Paul moves away from legalism (To-Do, Do-More, and Do-Better actions) and teaches about *license* (Can-Do actions). License is the opposite of legalism. License says, "*I can do what I want whenever I want and how much I want.*" Paul also addresses license in his first letter to the Corinthian church (see 1 Corinthians 10:23 in the margin). The Judaizers didn't trust in the real power of the gospel to transform hearts and minds and assumed that the gospel would give people permission to run wild and free.

Why do you think some Christians believe that because they are saved, they can act or live any way that they want to?

What are some clues or signs that believers are using grace as a justification to "sin first and ask for forgiveness later"?

What are some of the spiritual and practical consequences of seeing the gospel as license to live anyway that you want to?

There's an expanded discussion about spiritual license in Romans 6, as Paul also needed to teach the Romans about navigating their freedom in Christ:

[1] What shall we say, then? Shall we go on sinning so that grace may increase? [2] By no means! We are those who have died to sin; how can we live in it any longer?

[6]For we know that our old self was crucified with him so that the body ruled by sin might be done away with, that we should no longer be slaves to sin—[7]because anyone who has died has been set free from sin.

[11]In the same way, count yourselves dead to sin but alive to God in Christ Jesus. [12]Therefore do not let sin reign in your mortal body so that you obey its evil desires. [13]Do not offer any part of yourself to sin as an instrument of wickedness, but rather offer yourselves to God as those who have been brought from death to life; and offer every part of yourself to him as an instrument of righteousness. [14]For sin shall no longer be your master, because you are not under the law, but under grace.

(Romans 6:1-2, 6-7, 11-14 NIV)

Why is continuing to sin the opposite of what grace means in our lives? (vv. 1-2)

What are we free from? (v. 6)

How should we use our freedom? (v. 13)

What did grace do that the law couldn't do for us? (v. 14)

Once we say no to following rules, whether religious rules or our own self-imposed morality, we can be tempted to do whatever feels good to us, which usually distracts us from God's best for us. Instead, Paul challenges believers to serve each other in love.

Jesus gave a picture of serving others in love through the story of the Good Samaritan. He told this story because an expert in the law challenged Him with the question, "Teacher, . . . what must I do to inherit eternal life?" (Luke 10:25 NIV). Let's explore this a bit before jumping into the story.

Read Luke 10:27 and Matthew 22:37-40 in the sidebar. Underline all of the ways that we're supposed to love God.

According to Matthew 22:40, what does the law hang on?

[27]He answered, "'Love the Lord your God with all your heart and with all your soul and with all your strength and with all your mind'; and, 'Love your neighbor as yourself.'"

(Luke 10:27 NIV)

[37]Jesus replied: "'Love the Lord your God with all your heart and with all your soul and with all your mind.' [38]This is the first and greatest commandment. [39]And the second is like it: 'Love your neighbor as yourself.' [40]All the Law and the Prophets hang on these two commandments."

(Matthew 22:37-40 NIV)

The religious leader in Luke 10:27 knew Moses' law. His answer is proof that we can know something and still not live it out. Furthermore, in Matthew 22:40, Jesus affirms that the Jewish people knew the law was written so they could follow God faithfully. However, the religious leader who approached Jesus knew in his heart that he (the religious leader) didn't like some people.

This is why Jesus told the following story. As you read the story of the Good Samaritan, keep in mind what you know about the law, grace, and license. Also keep in mind that the three individuals in the story are metaphors for different groups of people: Priest (law keeper), Levite (religious person), Samaritan (one motivated by love).

Read Luke 10: 30-37, and answer the following questions.

Based on what you know about the law and religious hypocrisy, why do you think the priest and the Levite passed by the injured man?

It's one thing to be *nice* to someone. But what kind of behavior did the Samaritan demonstrate? What did he do to illustrate the command "love your neighbor as yourself"?

At the end of the story, we find a description of a neighbor. What is it? (v. 37)

As you reflect on this story and the people in your life who are hard to love, what are some takeaways for you?

Aside from the trap that the law would set for the Galatians, Paul knew that both legalism and license would rob them of the security and satisfaction of a loving, guilt-free relationship with God and others. The same goes for you and me. Living in God's love and showing God's love to others is the best version of freedom in Christ. This is what a rich and satisfying life looks like, and this is my prayer for you and for me.

Prayer

Dear God, thank You again for my freedom, won for me by Christ. I am no longer a slave to sin! You have freed me not only from my sinful spiritual condition but also from being held captive by sinful desires. God, change my heart, mind, and soul so that I can experience the fullest freedom in You; in Jesus's name. Amen.

Day 3: The Promise of Power

At the beginning of this week's study, I mentioned my struggle with overeating as well as the freedom I found in relying on my relationship with God instead of rules. I've had to make peace with the fact that I may be fighting these battles the rest of my life.

It's okay for us to have to keep battling something. Some people believe that freedom can't exist in an area of our lives unless the problem, temptation, struggle, or habit is eradicated forever. But Paul demonstrates that this line of thinking is incorrect.

In 2 Corinthians 12:1-10, Paul writes about everything he had done as a messenger of the gospel. If there were a superstar checklist, Paul could have ticked all of the boxes. However, Paul says that in order to avoid becoming prideful, a messenger from Satan afflicted him with a thorn in the flesh. Why would God allow this?

In the Book of Job in the Old Testament, Satan asks God for permission to devastate Job's life, and God allows it, confident in the character of Job. We can infer that what Satan means for evil, God will use for good (Genesis 50:20; Job 42). A similar dynamic may be in place with Paul.

Read 2 Corinthians 12:8-9 in the margin. What did God say was enough for Paul?

Ah-ha Moment

Did you notice any ah-ha spiritual breakthrough moments in today's study, your prayer time, or your daily activities? If so, record that moment on the final page of this week's study (page 171).

Big Idea

You don't have to fix yourself!

[8] *Three times I pleaded with the Lord to take it away from me.* [9] *But he said to me, "My grace is sufficient for you, for my power is made perfect in weakness."*

(2 Corinthians 12:8-9 NIV)

What is/are the thorn(s) in your flesh?

Why do you think God allows some of our spiritual struggles to persist, even though we've tried to pray them away?

Here's the hard truth about some issues we face as believers: We will live with some struggles until we leave this earth. As much as I want my emotional eating struggles to disappear, they haven't. That doesn't mean that I don't trust God or that I'm not saved by God's grace. It just means that like Paul, it's my thorn in the flesh. I could get discouraged about it or I can choose to see this struggle as a vehicle that drives me back to God. As I experience victory, I give glory to God rather than give attention to myself. (Here's an important note: Allowing my relationship with God to lead me to freedom doesn't mean that I ignore the wisdom of exercising and eating healthy foods; it means that I don't rely on those things to manage my struggle.)

Read Galatians 5:16.

Who should guide our lives?

What is the promise that comes with a Spirit-guided life?

Don't rush over this. This may be a breakthrough moment for you. Did you capture the promise? When you allow God's Holy Spirit to guide your life, you will find freedom from what your sinful nature (the flesh) desires or craves—freedom from your sin and strongholds.

God's goal for your life isn't to make all of your problems go away. But when you allow the Spirit to fight for you, you'll experience victory. When you allow the Holy Spirit to guide your life, the result is holy living—even when there are occasional setbacks. Even when there are persistent pressures, seasonal resurgences, or surprise attacks, you can face them assured of ultimate victory in Jesus's name.

As you reflect on the promise in Galatians 5:16, where might this promise bring fresh hope and perhaps even a break-through moment in your life?

Read John 14:26 in the margin. How does the Holy Spirit guide our lives?

But when the Father sends the Advocate as my representative—that is, the Holy Spirit—he will teach you everything and will remind you of everything I have told you.

(John 14:26)

Think about what it might have been like for the Israelites to live under the law without the indwelling of the Holy Spirit. During that time, they saw some supernatural miracles such as God parting the Red Sea, God guiding them with a pillar of cloud during the day and a pillar of fire at night, and God providing daily manna from heaven. That was all pretty cool, right? However, they had to manage their internal battles without the power of the Holy Spirit within them. There were times when God empowered certain people with His Spirit to accomplish specific tasks, such as a craftsman named Bezalel whom God appointed to make items for the Israelites' tent of meeting and ark of the covenant (Exodus 31:1-5). Later, God's Spirit came upon a blind and chained Samson so that he could defeat 1,000 Philistines (Judges 15:14–15). And there are other examples.

Yet because of Christ's death and resurrection, we have the permanent gift of the Holy Spirit, who indwells us. In my own life, I can see the Holy Spirit continuing to transform my heart and mind from self-righteous legalism to Spirit-driven attitudes, behaviors, and character. And I recognize that it's a process.

Read Galatians 5:17. What is the tension that we face?

These two forces are constantly doing what with each other?

Extra Insight

"Holy living also ensures that we make wise choices. We behave with integrity, respond well to hardship, respect others who are different than us or are difficult to love, and so forth. All said, living a holy life protects us from self-inflicted, avoidable heartache."[10]

I want to do what is good, but I don't. I don't want to do what is wrong, but I do it anyway.

(Romans 7:19)

Read Romans 7:19 in the margin. What does Paul observe about his struggle?

Think about an on-going, persistent struggle, sin, or stronghold in your life. How is it a spiritual battle and not a will-power issue?

Think about what it feels like to stretch a rubber band between your fingers. When you stretch it wide, you can feel the tension. Some tension is good. Tension is what allows the rubber band to serve its purpose. But if you stretch a rubber band too far, it will break. A snapped band is as useless as a slack band. Similarly, when we are stretched by hard and heartbreaking circumstances, our powerful God can take what Satan meant for evil and use it for our good (Genesis 50:20; Romans 8:28). He will not allow us to snap or break beyond repair and restoration.

When have you felt like you were being "stretched" spiritually?

When have you felt that your stretching was bringing you closer to God?

When have you felt that the stretching was too much and you couldn't handle it?

Being stretched and experiencing the tension of struggles that may not go away isn't easy. If you're living with a spiritual, emotional, medical, or relational challenge that isn't going to change on this side of heaven, I want you to know that you are seen and loved today by God and by me.

It is not our purpose here to discuss why bad things happen to good people, although that is a valuable and important theological conversation (and there are many excellent resources available on the subject). However, answers to that question do not eliminate the reality that some stretching in our human experience is ugly and unfair. Yet, like Paul's thorn in the flesh (which scholars suspect was a debilitating ailment), God's grace for us even in the hard and horrifically heartbreaking is *always* enough.

Prayer

God, today I am feeling stretched by dealing with

_____.

When _____ happens or

I feel like _____, the stretching

feels almost too much to bear. Yet I choose to trust that Your

grace is enough for me to get through this. Help me to see

Your grace unfolding today; in Jesus's name. Amen.

Day 4: Have Mercy on Me, God

I love sermons about the kinds of sin that aren't a problem for me. I sit up straighter and smile. Nothing makes me feel better as a Christian than when I hear the pastor preach and I smugly say to myself, "Welp, that's not a problem for me." Then I think about the people I want to text and say, "Hey, are you coming to the late service today? I think you'll find the sermon helpful."

If there's anything that a legalistic Christian can see better than anything else in this world, it's someone else's sin. Can I get an amen?

In Luke 18, Jesus tells a story about a Pharisee and a tax collector "to some who were confident of their own righteousness and looked down on everyone else" (Luke 18:9 NIV). In this story, the Pharisee prays to God and exclaims all of the ways that he lives the good religious life. He ticks all of the "Are you a good Christian?" checkboxes by naming all the people he's better than, and then he really proves his "good Christian" status by reminding God that he fasts twice a week and tithes his income. As a long-time former church staff member, I can say that someone like this guy would be known and celebrated for their spiritual maturity.

Ah-ha Moment

Did you notice any ah-ha spiritual breakthrough moments in today's study, your prayer time, or your daily activities? If so, record that moment on the final page of this week's study (page 171).

Big Idea

Your mistakes cannot outrun God's mercy.

But then, Jesus shifts to the tax collector's prayer. In that culture, tax collectors were despised by the Jews for their collaboration with the Romans. In Jesus's story, the tax collector didn't even come near the Temple to pray:

"But the tax collector stood at a distance. He would not even look up to heaven, but beat his breast and said, 'God, have mercy on me, a sinner.'"

(*Luke* 18:13 NIV)

That tax collector's prayer moves me every time. Notice how short and simple his prayer is—no doubt in contrast to the long list of his sins likely running through his mind. What's so moving about Jesus's story is that the tax collector knew exactly what he'd done and asked for mercy anyway.

This is a rich story for us, especially if we've ever struggled with legalism. That tax collector knew he couldn't be righteous enough on his own to undo the sin in his life. However, rather than run from God, the tax collector courageously moved toward God and asked for mercy. Oh, that we all would have the humility of that tax collector!

For those of us who share my struggle with legalism, here's an interesting observation: Because we try so hard to please God, we're spiritually crushed when it seems that we've failed. In fact, our spiritual failure, whether it's not doing our Bible study or missing church, makes us want to run and hide from God or double up on our To-Do, Do-More, and Do-Better actions to make up for it.

But what if God doesn't care what we do when we fail but, instead, cares more about whether we're willing to receive His mercy? Isn't that part of what the gospel is about?

In my life, one of the most important distinctions I've had to make in finding freedom from legalism is the difference between *conviction* and *condemnation*. Conviction connects me back to the gospel, whereas condemnation causes me to do even more or, if I'm really crushed, to hide.

In today's study, we'll look at the results of following our sinful nature. While the consequences of following our flesh are dire, God lavishly showers us with mercy when we admit our sin. Because He wants us to experience spiritual freedom and connection with others, we're going to leave some space in today's study for a repentance and confession exercise.

Let's finish Jesus's story about the Pharisee and tax collector.

Read Luke 18:14. What did Jesus say about the outcome of the tax collector's prayer?

Why was the tax collector, who had admitted to so many wrongs, sent home righteous whereas the Pharisee, who seemed to have done a lot right, went home unrighteous?

Jesus's story about the tax collector and the Pharisee is a setup for Paul's hard confrontation of sin in Galatians 5:19-21. Here Paul lists the outcomes of following our human desires. He taught the Galatians about allowing the Holy Spirit to work in their lives because without sanctification, they would fall prey to their own human desires. That would be a tragedy for them emotionally, spiritually, and relationally. The same goes for us. When we feel the tension between living by the Spirit and giving in to our flesh, the battle is real. Though the Spirit wants us to cooperate with His work so that we might experience life and peace, our flesh also desires our "yes" but can only promise lots of guilt for a moment of pleasure.

Read both translations of Galatians 5:19-21 below and answer the questions that follow.

¹⁹ The acts of the flesh are obvious: sexual immorality, impurity and debauchery; ²⁰ idolatry and witchcraft; hatred, discord, jealousy, fits of rage, selfish ambition, dissensions, factions ²¹ and envy; drunkenness, orgies, and the like. I warn you, as I did before, that those who live like this will not inherit the kingdom of God. (NIV)

¹⁹⁻²¹ It is obvious what kind of life develops out of trying to get your own way all the time: repetitive, loveless, cheap sex; a stinking accumulation of mental and emotional garbage; frenzied and joyless grabs for happiness; trinket gods; magic-show religion; paranoid loneliness; cutthroat competition; all-consuming-yet-never-satisfied wants; a brutal temper; an impotence to love or be loved; divided homes and divided lives; small-minded and lopsided pursuits; the vicious habit of depersonalizing everyone into a rival; uncontrolled and uncontrollable addictions; ugly parodies of community. I could go on. This isn't the first time I have warned you, you know. If you use your freedom this way, you will not inherit God's kingdom. (MSG)

Which of the outcomes described have you seen in your life? Put a checkmark beside them.

What are some of the sins that "good Christians" might be tempted to minimize or hide?

Ultimately, what will happen to those who follow acts of the flesh?

Scholars note that Paul's list is divided into four categories: sex, religion, relationships, and indulgences.[11] What's also important is that Paul does not limit the list of outcomes to just what he has written here. The end of the list in Galatians 5:21 in the New Living Translation says, "…and other sins like these." For rule-followers who want to judge others or license-lovers who want to see how close to sin they can get, Paul's main point is that *all* flesh-driven desires lead us away from the freedom in Christ we are meant to enjoy.

In your opinion, what are some other possible desires that Paul could have listed?

Now, for those of us who are rule-followers, verses such as these can make us feel even more strict and diligent in our rule-following behavior, because we don't want to be like "those" people. Yet we *are* those people. None of us is perfect.

What are some of the sins and shortcomings that are hard for you to confess?

Depending on your life experience, reading the previous verses may trigger guilt, shame, or condemnation. Please do not entertain any lies that say God hasn't or won't forgive you or that you'll never change. The power of the gospel is that you don't have to save yourself. Jesus has done the saving work for you; and as you live in Christ, you can be assured that you will become more and more like Christ.

Confession and Repentance

We began today's study with Jesus's story about the Pharisee and tax collector partly because I wanted to lay a foundation for God's mercy and forgiveness, especially if you've made some mistakes in life that you're afraid, ashamed, or unwilling to talk about. I'd like to create some space for you to talk about any unconfessed sin with God today. This is a safe space, especially if you've never done this before.

Here are two important reminders: 1) *You can't outrun God's mercy for your life.* 2) *You don't have to earn God's mercy either.* Whether you checked every single sin in Galatians 5:19-21 or you only checked one, God's mercy and forgiveness are the same for all of us.

> **Right now, reflect on whatever you're feeling in your heart and soul. Which do you feel?**
>
> ___ **Conviction – Admitting your sin and drawing near to God**
>
> ___ **Condemnation – Admitting your sin and running from God**

If you're feeling conviction, meaning that you see your sin and you want God's forgiveness, you're on the right track. If you're feeling condemnation, I'm praying hard that what follows will help any feelings of condemnation to fall away.

> **Read the Scriptures in the margin.**
>
> **What does 1 John 1:9 promise those who confess their sins?**
>
> **What does Romans 8:1 promise those who are in Christ Jesus?**

The Bible refers to David as a man after God's own heart—despite his sin. In the Old Testament, he committed adultery with a woman named Bathsheba. Not only that, but he arranged for her husband to be killed in

Extra Insight

"Those who come by grace alone are new people. While they still wrestle with sin, the flesh will not dominate them. They have new desires and new power to live. Our good works don't save us, but true salvation leads to fruitfulness and faithfulness."[12]

If we confess our sins, he is faithful and just and will forgive us our sins and purify us from all unrighteousness.
(1 John 1:9 NIV)

Therefore, there is now no condemnation for those who are in Christ Jesus.
(Romans 8:1 NIV)

Ah-ha Moment

Did you notice any ah-ha spiritual breakthrough moments in today's study, your prayer time, or your daily activities? If so, record that moment on the final page of this week's study (page 171).

battle to cover up his sin. To make matters worse, King David tried to hide his sin until the prophet Nathan confronted him (2 Samuel 12). Eventually, the toll of David's sin wore him down and he confessed. Scholars believe Psalm 51 is David's confession and repentance of his sin.

This psalm is a beautiful prayer that you can use in your own life, especially when you realize that God is prompting you to turn away from sin or behaviors that tempt you toward sin. Let's end today by adapting the psalm as a personal confession.

Prayer

Use Psalm 51:1-17 (NIV) to construct your own confession. Personalize each line of the psalm according to your situation or feelings. You can also rewrite the desired lines in your own words in the space beside them. Then pray your prayer aloud to God.

¹ *Have mercy on me, O God,*

    according to your unfailing love;

according to your great compassion

    blot out my transgressions.

² *Wash away all my iniquity*

    and cleanse me from my sin.

³ *For I know my transgressions,*

    and my sin is always before me.

⁴ *Against you, you only, have I sinned*

    and done what is evil in your sight;

so you are right in your verdict

    and justified when you judge.

⁵ *Surely I was sinful at birth,*

    sinful from the time my mother conceived me.

⁶ *Yet you desired faithfulness even in the womb;*

    you taught me wisdom in that secret place.

⁷ *Cleanse me with hyssop, and I will be clean;*

    wash me, and I will be whiter than snow.

⁸ Let me hear joy and gladness;

  let the bones you have crushed rejoice.

⁹ Hide your face from my sins

  and blot out all my iniquity

¹⁰ Create in me a pure heart, O God,

  and renew a steadfast spirit within me.

¹¹ Do not cast me from your presence.

  or take your Holy Spirit from me.

¹² Restore to me the joy of your salvation

  and grant me a willing spirit, to sustain me.

¹³ Then I will teach transgressors your ways,

  so that sinners will turn back to you.

¹⁴ Deliver me from the guilt of bloodshed, O God,

  you who are God my Savior,

  and my tongue will sing of your righteousness.

¹⁵ Open my lips, Lord,

  and my mouth will declare your praise.

¹⁶ You do not delight in sacrifice, or I would bring it;

  you do not take pleasure in burnt offerings.

¹⁷ My sacrifice, O God, is a broken spirit;

  a broken and contrite heart

  you, God, will not despise.

God, as Your daughter, I am not condemned, but as I confess my sin before You, I ask for Your mercy and receive it; in Jesus's name. Amen.

Day 5: Fruit of the Spirit

Whenever I travel to Honduras on a mission trip, I enjoy fresh mangoes plucked right from the trees in my host family's front yard. The mangoes in my grocery store at home are fine, but the Honduran mangoes are three times the size and, best of all, free!

Big Idea

The fruit of the Spirit shows us what Christ is like in our lives.

I can't explain how much I enjoy eating those giant, fresh mangoes. Many times, I eat only mango for breakfast or lunch because the fragrant fruit tastes so fresh and satisfying.

Today we're going to be exploring spiritual fruit. After going through the list of sinful desires, Paul closes out Galatians 5 by talking about the evidence of a Spirit-led life, what we call the fruit of the Spirit. However, for a long time I thought Paul meant "fruits" of the Spirit, plural, rather than "fruit," singular.

If you have studied the fruit of the Spirit before, great! This teaching is like the gospel—you can never hear it often enough. And if you've never studied the fruit of the Spirit before, I pray you find this experience as sweet and satisfying as those Honduran mangoes!

Write Galatians 5:22–23 below, listing the nine attributes of the fruit of Spirit on the lines provided. (Definitions of the individual attributes are below.)

1._____   4._____   7._____

2._____   5._____   8._____

3._____   6._____   9._____

Love – "to serve someone for their good and intrinsic value"[13]

Joy – "happiness not dependent on our circumstances"[14]

Peace –"tranquility of heart"[15]

Patience – "courageous endurance without quitting"[16]

Kindness - an inner secureness that enables one to "serve others in a practical way"[17]

Goodness – "love in action"[18]

Faithfulness – "dependability and loyalty" to Christ[19]

Gentleness – "a teachable attitude"[20]

Self-Control – "ability to withstand human desires that are apart from God"[21]

Why do you think Paul calls these nine attributes the fruit of the Spirit?

Take a moment to label each of the nine attributes of the fruit of the Spirit listed on the previous page according to its presence in your life, writing the appropriate number beside each:

1 (not present)
2 (barely present)
3 (sometimes present)
4 (frequently present)
5 (almost always present)

What are your thoughts as you look at the results?

Are there some spiritual struggles in your life that you can connect to the lack of certain attributes of the fruit of the Spirit?

You may have noticed that the attributes of the fruit of the Spirit are listed above in three columns. That's because scholars have noted the following:

- The first triad = relationship between us and God (love, joy, peace)
- The second triad = relationship between us and others (patience, kindness, goodness)
- The third triad = these develop as our relationship with God develops (faithfulness, gentleness, self-control)[22]

Why does Paul teach the Galatians about the fruit of the Spirit? Since he outlined what our human desires produce, it makes sense for him to contrast those tragedies with what the life-giving power of the Holy Spirit produces in our lives when we cooperate with the Spirit in the process of sanctification. Additionally, while Paul's teachings about the law reminded the Galatians that outward acts can never result in inward righteousness, the fruit of the Spirit was the *evidence* that they were becoming more like Christ in their attitudes, behaviors, and character.

Realizing that the fruit of the Spirit is evidence of sanctification led to a breakthrough moment for me. I can use the fruit of the Spirit to discern whether I'm engaging in a spiritual discipline or activity because I'm trying to check off a to-do list (rules-oriented) or because I want to connect with or obey God (relationship-oriented). If I'm listening to worship music, serving others, giving, or reading my Bible because I want the Spirit to transform my character, that's good. But if I'm doing those things because I feel like I can gain points with God, that mindset needs to be challenged.

Can you recall an experience when you sensed that the Holy Spirit was working on one or more of the attributes of the fruit of the Spirit in your life? If so, describe it briefly:

How did you cooperate with the Holy Spirit's work in your life?

Since the Holy Spirit's power is needed to transform our attitudes, behavior, and character and make us more like Christ, our role is to cooperate with the Spirit. This means that we listen for the Spirit's leading and position ourselves in experiences that allow us to spend time learning and living like Jesus.

I remember a season when I sensed the Holy Spirit was working on kindness in me. I'm naturally optimistic, positive, and nice, but that's not the same thing as the spiritual definition of kindness, which is a Spirit-enabled pleasant inward attitude toward others. You see, I could look really nice on the outside, but if someone wasn't doing what I wanted, I would get really angry and ugly on the inside. This meant that my smile was fake—even though I will acknowledge that my fakeness allowed me to maintain self-control.

It was time for my insides to match my outsides.

As I was doing my Bible study one day, I came across Proverbs 16:24: "Kind words are like honey— / sweet to the soul and healthy for the body." Immediately, I sensed that was a verse I needed to focus on. I wrote the verse on a notecard and quickly memorized it. Then, I turned it into a prayer that I prayed each day for an entire year.

God, give me kind words, a kind heart, and a kind attitude.

Additionally, that verse became my prayer before every meeting, phone call, and conversation with my kids or other family members. As I continued to pray and ask God for help applying His Word regularly in my life, I noticed

that God's Spirit began reshaping my interior responses. In time, I noticed that when people didn't meet my expectations, I didn't bluster inwardly. Instead, my outward smile matched my inward smile. I couldn't have done that on my own! Furthermore, I noticed that as kindness was growing in me, that intentional focus on letting the Spirit lead me also brought growth in the other attributes of the fruit of the Spirit.

I hope this story encourages you, especially if you feel like you're failing when it comes to one or more aspects of the fruit of the Spirit. Remember, God won't give up on you! One scholar offers these encouraging words: "If someone has the Spirit in them—if they are a Christian—the fruit will grow."[23] Be encouraged today!

Is there an attribute of the fruit of the Spirit that you sense needs some extra focus? The following exercise is an opportunity for you to allow the Holy Spirit to do some intentional work, especially if you feel prompted by God or by feedback from others.

Fruit of the Spirit Challenge

While the fruit of the Spirit should be fully evident in our lives, the Spirit is at work on each attribute in different ways.

Pick one attribute of the fruit of the Spirit and write it here:

_____

Find a Bible verse that speaks to this attribute, and write it below:

Turn the verse into a short prayer, writing it below:

Ah-ha Moment

Did you notice any ah-ha spiritual breakthrough moments in today's study, your prayer time, or your daily activities? If so, record that moment on the final page of this week's study (page 171).

Work on memorizing the verse and repeating your prayer each day for the next three days. Notice when you're doing it because you desire God's transformation and when you're doing it just because you said that you would. What insights do you gain?

Any insights or observations about your experience? Write them below:

Just as my favorite juicy, fragrant Honduran mangoes need time to grow, so the fruit of the Spirit needs time to grow in our lives. As we grow, the emerging sweetness of what the Spirit is doing in our lives will be a powerful testimony to the gospel—and a blessing to us as well.

Prayer

Dear God, just as You cause earthly fruit to grow, I trust that Your Spirit is growing the fruit of the Spirit within me. I will let go of trying to make improvements on my own, and I will trust Your Spirit to cultivate a real and lasting transformation within me so that my spiritual growth is a sweet testimony to Your glory, not my self-effort; in Jesus's name. Amen.

Weekly Breakthrough Reflection Exercise

Each day this week you have been prompted to record on this page any ah-ha spiritual breakthrough moments you've had in your study, prayer time, or daily activities. Take time now to reflect once more on where you've seen God working in your heart, mind, and life this week, and add any other ah-ha moments below.

Lightbulb
You gain new understanding about God or yourself.

Describe the moment:

_____
_____
_____

Butterfly
You surrender or let go of a struggle, sin, or stronghold from your past.

Describe the moment:

_____
_____
_____

Rainbow
You find new or renewed hope based on God's promises for your life.

Describe the moment:

_____
_____
_____

Busted Brick Wall
You confront and face up to any kind of fear or worry.

Describe the moment:

_____
_____
_____

Line in the Sand
You realize that a sin, struggle, or stronghold is no longer acceptable.

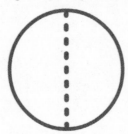

Describe the moment:

_____
_____
_____

Split-the-Rock
You have a supernatural shift in your faith or circumstances after faithfully praying and letting God lead.

Describe the moment:

_____
_____
_____

Choose one of your ah-ha moments from the previous page and describe it here:

What is a spiritual breakthrough you're still praying for?

Option: Write a prayer below:

Video Viewer Guide
WEEK 5

Scriptures: Galatians 5:1, Galatians 5:17, Galatians 5:22-23, Galatians 5:25-26

We want to stay _____, but there's also this other side that feels like it is _____ us.

There's a difference between _____ and _____.

Spiritual practices are what put you in position to be _____ by God.

Freedom Principle #5

Spiritual breakthrough is an ah-ha moment when we _____ that God is at work within us, _____ what He's doing, and _____ to it.

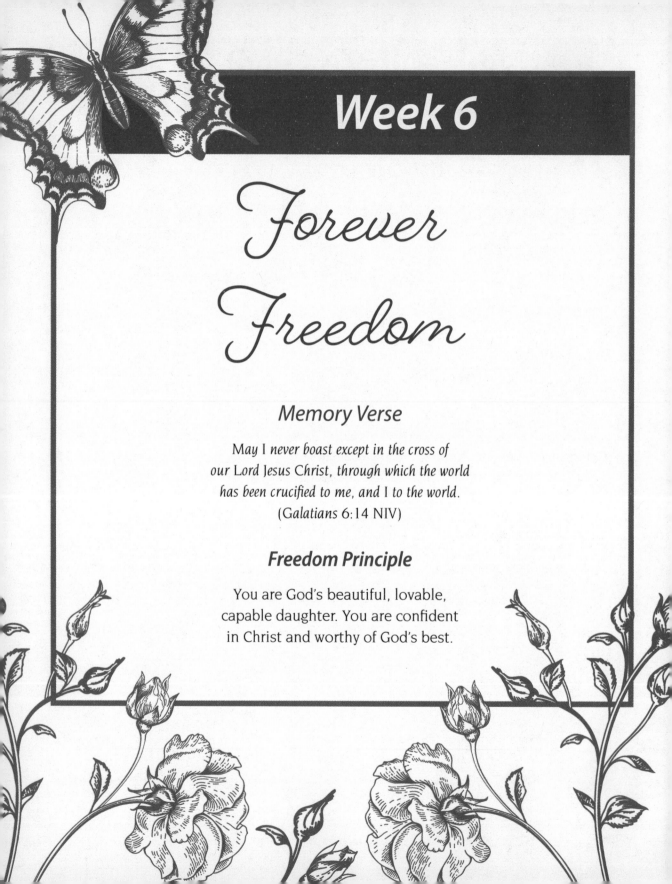

Forever Freedom

Memory Verse

May I never boast except in the cross of our Lord Jesus Christ, through which the world has been crucified to me, and I to the world.
(Galatians 6:14 NIV)

Freedom Principle

You are God's beautiful, lovable, capable daughter. You are confident in Christ and worthy of God's best.

When I began writing this *Breakthrough* Bible study, I prayed that God would use this study to reach women who fear that they are never good enough for God; or stuck in a frustrating cycle of To-Do, Do-More, or Do-Better actions because of guilt; or stalled in their faith because of emotional or relational wounds inflicted by others. Whether or not any of those situations applies to you, Paul's teachings to the Galatians remind us all of the power of the gospel in our lives each and every day. The gospel empowers us to walk in freedom in Christ so that we can live and love like Jesus and experience the great adventure of faith that God has for us.

As we begin our final week of study, let's recap the freedom principles we've explored over the past five weeks:

- The gospel is based on God's perfect promises, not our (or others') performance.
- A relationship with God means that we receive from Him rather than follow rules for Him.
- Freedom in Christ is living free from fear and fully alive with joy and purpose.
- Your freedom in Christ cannot be shaken or taken away by anyone who chooses not to live like Christ.
- Spiritual breakthrough is an ah-ha moment when we recognize that God is at work within us, receive what He's doing, and respond to it.

Take a moment and circle the freedom principles above that resonate with you most right now. Now, reflect on why they connect with you. As we move into the last week of our time together, I continue to pray that you receive and relax into the realities of the gospel message: God's love for you is based on His promises, not any performance-based things you do—even good things like Bible study and prayer.

This week we'll wrap up our study by looking at the last part of Paul's letter to the Galatians. Our final freedom principle is this:

- You are God's beautiful, lovable, capable daughter. You are confident in Christ and worthy of God's best.

We will focus on how the gospel gives us life, freedom, and confidence in our relationship with God and our relationships with others, particularly other believers. If you've ever struggled in relationships with other Christians, this week's study will encourage, inspire, and equip you to pursue healthy, whole, biblical relationships with others.

Day 1: Helping Others without Hurting Yourself

While walking at a park, a couple in front of me abruptly stepped off the path. The woman reached down to take off her shoe as the man moved his body closer so that she could lean against him for stability. Turns out, she had a rock in her shoe. It only took her a few seconds to pluck out the rock and put her shoe back on. He held on to her while she took off her shoe, and then she grabbed on to him as she put the shoe back on.

As I watched that little scene unfold, I was reminded of the times when I've been like that woman with something in my life that caused me discomfort or pain. I've felt emotional stones in my life such as depression, anxiety, control issues, anger, and disappointment. Emotional stones hurt! But it's much harder to remove our emotional, spiritual, or relational stones if we don't have others to lean on.

Now, imagine that same scene, except this time the man criticizes the woman when she leans against him. How would she feel trying to get the rock out of her shoe on her own while he stands there complaining that if she'd been more careful or smarter, she wouldn't have gotten into that situation?

Unfortunately, we Christians often have the reputation of being inclined to judge and criticize instead of offer support when someone reveals an "emotional stone" or "sin stone" in his or her life. As we will see today, Paul's teaching in Galatians 6 has to do with this point—and I believe the fact that he addresses it in the final part of his letter is significant. Let's explore why.

Read Galatian 6:1. Is Paul's instruction directed to believers or nonbelievers?

What is the goal of Paul's instruction in this verse?

R_____

When Paul writes about restoring someone who's fallen into sin, the original language refers to how a physician resets a broken bone. If you've ever broken a bone, you know how painful it is. When a broken bone is unattended, it can still mend back together, but the healing process takes much longer and the healed bone is often weaker than before.

Galatians 6:1 calls us as believers living in Spirit-led community to surround those who have fallen into sin and brokenness and to stand close beside them in the healing process. When we stand by believers who have a stone stuck in their spiritual lives or who have fallen into sin, we get the privilege of seeing God work in their lives. However, if we look at their sin or struggle with jumping through To-Do, Do-More, or Do-Better hoops, we will become impatient with them.

What are some examples of standing beside and supporting another believer who has fallen into sin? Include an example from your own life, if possible—whether you were the one who fell or the one who stood beside another.

Extra Insight

"Only the gospel makes us neither self-confident nor self-disdaining, but both bold and humble."[1]

At the end of verse 1, what is Paul's warning?

Paul begins with the reality that, as believers, we are not going to live perfect lives. Perhaps you or someone you know has faced a season in life when sin stole the show. I love that Paul equips godly believers with wisdom and instruction on how to pursue a believer who can't or won't get out of their sin struggle on their own.

So, why is Paul talking about this now in the final chapter of his letter to the Galatians? The timing is important!

Until this point, Paul has been refuting the teaching of the Judaizers about extra requirements for the gospel. Consider how those false teachings created a toxic culture in their church. When people elevate rules over relationship, personal connections and community are always ruined.

Let's looks at the three parts of Paul's teaching in Galatians 6:1-2.

1. The goal of the gospel is restoration (freedom in Christ), not making someone follow rules.

As Paul talks about confronting believers who were trapped or caught in sin, it's possible that the Galatians who were influenced by the Judaizers might have used their toxic teaching as a way to reinforce the importance of following rules rather than as a message of restoration. I can imagine that if someone wasn't following the rules, those same "Judaized Galatians" might have run after them with stones in their hands, just as the Pharisees were fond of doing in Jesus's time.

One key takeaway for me is that the best way to combat toxic church culture is to elevate the fruit of the Spirit in our individual and communal lives, especially when communicating with each other.

> **How can allowing the fruit of the Spirit to lead our conversation help us to avoid toxic relationships and church culture?**

It's hard to see someone trapped in a destructive sin. But we can be lights for the gospel in someone's dark situation! We don't need to shame them or pressure them to jump through the Do-Better self-improvement hoop because we trust God's power to transform them from the inside out.

2. Spirit-led gentleness should guide our conversations, comments, and questions.

In Galatians 6:1, Paul writes that believers should "gently and humbly" help someone who is caught in sin to get back to the right path. Other translations say "restore that person gently" (NIV) and "should restore him in a spirit of gentleness" (ESV).

As one who has been in the church all of my life, I've seen too many instances where well-meaning believers confronted a sin-trapped believer with shaming words, condemnation, and threats. Perhaps you've seen one of these confrontations. It generally never ends well.

Romans 2:4 teaches that God's kindness turns us away from sin. If God doesn't blast us with condemning words and spewed anger in our sin, then we shouldn't do it to others. This is why Paul includes the need for gentleness. One scholar writes, "If we do feel we are above the person, our air of superiority will come through and we will destroy, not restore."[2]

Complete the following chart:

Indicators that someone is handling confrontation with gentleness:	Indicators that someone is handling confrontation with legalism/pride:

Just as Paul taught the Galatians that God would restore their relationship with Him through love, not legalism, so he wanted them to apply that same approach to their Christian community.

Years ago, a ministry leader contacted me about someone on the team who had fallen into sin as the result of a personal decision. As the executive leader for the team, it seemed to me that the most efficient answer was to make a phone call and say, "Hey, you know that's sin. Stop doing that. Get it together." But rather than shoot off an email requiring a behavior change, I set up a face-to-face meeting in my office. I sat on my sofa and asked the person a series of questions that conveyed I cared about what was going on in their life, not just the situation.

As a long-time church staffer and ministry leader, God has taught me that my first responsibility as a leader is to lead with love, not legalism. This means that I should never use my influence to intimidate people, especially those who are struggling. The goal isn't to fix people so that I can feel better about being an effective Christian or leader. The goal is to point people to the life-giving power of the gospel so that they may experience freedom in Christ.

In your opinion, what are some reasons why Christians try to fix each other with rules or legalism instead of Spirit-led relationship?

When believers demonstrate Spirit-led attitudes when confronting and restoring another believer, what message about the gospel does that send to others—both believers and nonbelievers?

During that face-to-face meeting in my office, my questions opened up a conversation about the individual's life and spiritual journey. I learned about some contributing factors that led to the outcome that had drawn the ministry leader's attention. Fixing the "appearance" issue wasn't as important as the internal restoration needing to take place. As God's Spirit worked that day, I watched how the fruit of the Spirit ministered to that individual in ways that scolding, shame, or rules never could. I saw how the Spirit-led conversation changed the atmosphere around them. I prayed that they would begin listening to the Holy Spirit within, but I also knew I wasn't in control of what happened next. When the individual left my office that day, there were no guarantees; in fact, nothing on the exterior of the situation had changed.

Within a few months, the person made some radical decisions to walk toward God's best for their life. One of the sweetest moments happened when I ran into this person a year later and discovered they were smiling, serving at church, and growing in their faith. They thanked me for taking the time to sit with them that day. Though they had been scared and ashamed about the situation, they felt God's Spirit working within them during our conversation.

Here are some questions or statements I have developed over many years of talking with other believers who are in the midst of sin that can help us approach difficult conversations with gentleness and the ultimate goal of restoration:

- I care about you, and I'm praying God's best blessing for your life.
- Where do you feel close to God? Is there a place where you feel far from God?
- Can you tell me what's been hard about this for you?
- I've seen...I've noticed...(Share firsthand observations, not opinions or speculation.)
- What do you think God's best blessing is for you in this situation?
- I'd like to connect you with a mentor you can check in with for the next few months. Is that okay?

What are some other statements or questions that you could use to talk and walk with another believer in need of restoration?

Our goal is always to point people back to the power of the gospel rather than attempt to fix them by giving out a list of To-Do, Do-More, or Do-Better rules. Not only is reminding them of the gospel's power best for them, but pointing them gently to the gospel protects us from shaming or scolding them.

3. When you're helping someone, don't harm yourself.

There are many ways well-meaning believers can start out helping someone only to end up hurting themselves. This can happen when the emphasis is placed on rescuing someone rather than on encouraging Spirit-led restoration. Fear or frustration can undermine a gentle attitude, or pride can emerge. When that happens, a person might get angry or bitter that the person they are trying to help isn't responding or "being fixed" as a result of their tremendous effort. I've been guilty of this in the past.

In one mentoring relationship, I spent a lot of time with the mentee. We would talk and pray together. She was honest about some of the strongholds in her life. I really wanted to help her find freedom from those strongholds; however, mounting frustration and bitterness in my heart revealed that what I wanted for her had begun to overtake my desire for the Spirit to work in her.

For those who serve as a Bible study or small group leader, lay minister, ministry team leader, or recovery ministry volunteer, it's vital to have accountability friends as trusted voices to call attention to any ongoing frustration, burnout, or bitterness.

> **Reread Galatians 6:1-2. Now consider a relationship with another believer in which you have the opportunity to encourage the process of restoration. As you reflect on Paul's instruction, do you sense something you need to say or do with this individual? If so, write a prayer below, asking God for help:**

We must never forget that the God who raised Jesus from the dead is the same God whose power is at work in the life of a person caught in sin. Our job isn't to shame people back to God; rather, we should stand next to them, offering a shoulder to lean on if they need it. If we believe that God is really in control, then we don't have to try to force people to follow rules in hopes of "fixing" them.

Prayer

God, remind me that You are responsible for life change, not me. You've called me to love and lead people to You. Help me to share Your gospel of grace as the only way to true freedom—and more effective than any self-help method out there. Thank You that I can trust Your power to transform willing lives; in Jesus's name. Amen.

Day 2: Giving Gospel Grace to Each Other

Big Idea

The gospel equips us to give grace and truth to each other.

Years ago, I traveled to speak at a women's event. My lovely hostess sponsored a breakfast gathering with some of the pastors' wives in the area the day before the event. As we sat around the large table enjoying a beautiful breakfast buffet, we talked about our families and faith. Since a main ministry focus at the time was small groups, I asked the women about their individual small group experiences.

Silence.

Not just quiet, but an uneasy, uncomfortable quiet.

It took a few moments, but the women told me that as pastors' wives, they didn't feel they were safe talking about what was really going on in their lives and families. They didn't want to share their parenting or marriage struggles out of fear that they would embarrass their husbands or that other women would shame them for not "having it together." I listened to those women, and we brainstormed some ideas about how they could create safe spaces to be honest and vulnerable with each other.

Years before, I had felt the same as those women. In my *Surrendered* Bible study, I wrote about the summer day when I broke down sobbing at my women's Bible study meeting, finally telling the truth about some personal struggles with anxiety and perfectionism. After my breakdown, one of the women sent me a text to thank me for showing up and being real with them that day. She'd assumed that because I had a leadership role and looked put together, I didn't have the same struggles that she did.

Read Galatians 6:2. What are we to do for each other?

What do you think carrying, sharing, or bearing our problems with each other has to do with the "law of Christ"?

In your experience, how has sharing your problems with another believer increased your connection with that person?

Extra Insight

"Law of Christ" in Galatians 6:2 means that we're to love our neighbors as ourselves.[3]

In Galatians 6:2, the Greek word "carry" is *bastazó*,[4] which means "to bear the physical, emotional or spiritual load threatening to crush his fellow believers."[5] Think about that for a moment. Paul isn't just telling believers that they are to sit politely across from someone over a cup of coffee. Rather, the imagery of the word *bastazó* seems to paint a picture of us contending with our hearts, minds, and souls for those who are caught in the trap of sin. As Tim Keller says, "You cannot help with a burden unless you come very close to a burdened person."[6]

Can you recall a time when you showed up to share the burden with someone who was weighed down by a personal tragedy or illness or caught in sin? If so, describe it briefly:

Does Paul mean for us to carry someone's load in a way that removes their personal responsibility or the consequences of their sin? No. He teaches about that a few verses later. Unlike the Pharisees who essentially tried to put individual legalistic yokes on people to weigh them down spiritually, Paul teaches that our freedom in Christ gives us free shoulders to come alongside believers who are weighed down by sins.

Perhaps we should stop being shocked when we hear of a believer who has had an affair or has been caught embezzling. Often our shock, outrage, and disappointment come from the fact that we'd never do such a thing, so how could they? Maybe you don't think that way, but there was a time when my legalistic mindset was quick to judge other Christians who fell into sin. Should we treat sin lightly? Absolutely not! But what if we took the emphasis off our shock and disappointment and used our energy to actually show up and love the people who have gotten a "sin rock" in their shoe and need someone give them a shoulder to lean on?

He comforts us in all our troubles so that we can comfort others. When they are troubled, we will be able to give them the same comfort God has given us.
(2 Corinthians 1:4)

Read 2 Corinthians 1:4 in the margin. Our approach to being there for others should be fueled by whom?

How does standing with someone who is struggling or caught in sin reinforce community?

One of the best ways for us to be there before, during, and after such moments in others' lives is participating in Bible study or other small groups. As a Bible study and small group leader for almost two decades, I've been privileged to show up and help carry the load when jobs were lost, marriages fell apart, children rebelled, surgeries were scheduled, suicide was attempted, and much more. Recently, I got a phone call from a friend who was overwhelmed by a serious emergency. She apologized for calling and burdening me with her news. However, for me, it has been a privilege to pray for my sister in Christ.

Is there someone in your life who is carrying a heavy load on her own? If so, what are some simple ways that you can reach out and share her load?

There's more going on in our Bible study groups than just reading our Bibles. As we talk together about God's Word and what's going on in our lives, our hearts and minds are moving toward freedom together.

Read James 5:16 in the margin. What happens when we confess our sins to each other?

What are some reasons that you or other Christians feel afraid or even embarrassed about sharing your struggles or sin?

Too often, we hide our spiritual dirty laundry from others out of fear, shame, guilt, or embarrassment. We don't want others to find out. This fear response activates a part of our brain called the amygdala, which is responsible for our fight, flight, or freeze mode. God created this important function to kick in whenever there's a danger that requires an instant physical response. However, when our amygdala stays fired up out of stress or fear, it can get in the way of our healthy decision-making. Various researchers report that putting our problems into words actually reduces our fears and lowers our stress. The data also indicates that therapy, journaling, and other forms of talking about one's struggles have a positive effect on immunity and mental health.[7]

Confess your sins to each other and pray for each other so that you may be healed. The earnest prayer of a righteous person has great power and produces wonderful results.

(James 5:16)

Read Galatians 6:3. What message does Paul convey to those who feel they have it together?

In verse 3, it appears that Paul aims to call out those who champion the "pull yourself up by your boot straps" philosophy of personal responsibility. Legalism puts its nose in the air and says, "Well, that's your problem to figure out," or, "If you were more like me, you wouldn't have gotten into that mess." Legalism doesn't like to get dirty with other people's problems.

However, just because the gospel saves us doesn't mean we don't fall into a self-inflicted pit of sin or pain from time to time. We need our brothers and sisters in Christ to throw us a lifeline rooted in the life-giving gospel and pull a little so that we can climb our way out.

Last week we studied the story of the Good Samaritan. If you recall, both a priest and a Levite saw the injured man and passed him by before the Samaritan stopped to offer help. Imagine yourself as the Samaritan. What would it have been like to pick up the injured man from the side of the road and carry him to a place where he could receive care? Chances are you would have gotten blood on your clothes and probably a few sore muscles from bearing the man's weight on your body.

Still, the Samaritan stopped his agenda to save the life of another.

Read Galatians 6:4-5. What are the main points Paul is making in these verses?

Here Paul shifts from talking about helping others carry their unbearable burdens to each person being responsible for their own load. Paul actually uses two different words to distinguish between burdens and loads. A burden is a heavy weight, but a load is like a backpack.

It's here that Paul reaffirms his teaching on not comparing our Christian journey to anyone else's. Though God allows the circumstances in our lives, He can use them all to draw us closer to Him. We all experience different levels of heartache, pain, and difficulty. No human is exempt. However, it's like apples and oranges when we compare our pain, sin tendencies, or sensitives to those of another, because we are all different and our situations are complex.

Paul teaches that we've got to keep our eyes on our own Hula-Hoop when it comes to walking out our faith. When we see someone else's problems and assume that we could have managed that problem better, that's pride. It's also prideful to look at our own problems and get mad at others for having seemingly easier, less stressful problems. In both cases, our focus is on ourselves and not on God.

How have you compared the struggles and difficulties of your life or spiritual journey to others?

How have those comparisons impacted your faith or how you feel about other Christians?

What can you do to stop comparing and shift your focus back to your own spiritual journey?

Getting involved in the lives of other Christians and living out the gospel isn't easy, but it is worth it! Let's pay attention to big and small ways we can share the burdens of other Christians. We might send a card, make (or order) a meal, take someone out for coffee, or sit down to have a difficult but important conversation about sin. No matter what we do, God's calling is the same for each of us: *We are to show up and support our Christian sisters and brothers who are struggling, whether or not we think they deserve it.*

Ah-ha Moment

Did you notice any ah-ha spiritual breakthrough moments in today's study, your prayer time, or your daily activities? If so, record that moment on the final page of this week's study (page 201).

Prayer

Dear God, plenty of Christians around me need someone to walk beside them and share their burden. While it's time-consuming, inconvenient, and difficult to show up and share the load, I want to be obedient to what You've called me to do. I will be sensitive to the Holy Spirit's promptings to say "yes" to helping someone in need; in Jesus's name. Amen.

Day 3: Harvest of Blessing

Big Idea

The gospel equips us to give grace and truth to each other.

I love shopping at my local farmers' market! Each weekend, my eyes feast upon the tables of vibrant colors of the fruits and vegetables. My stomach grumbles in anticipation of how good those gorgeous creations of God will taste in my mouth.

Who knew that a farmers' market could stir beauty and inspiration in my soul each week? My eyes feast on the endless rows of fruits and vegetables of different colors, shapes, and sizes. While my local grocery stores carry the same produce, there is something powerful about seeing the people who grew those fruits and vegetables standing proudly behind them and then offering them to me. I don't have the gift of gardening, but I'm still in awe of how tiny little seeds can grow and multiply into such beauty, goodness, and purpose.

The same is true of the fruit of the Holy Spirit in each of us—it grows and multiplies into such beauty, goodness, and purpose. A gift of the gospel is that we get to see how God works through us. While God can accomplish any and all things without our help, the Holy Spirit working within us transforms us in such a way that we can't help but impact the people around us. When we live free in Christ, our lives produce the fruit of the Spirit that inspires and nourishes others.

Today we will explore Paul's teaching on the spiritual concepts of reaping and sowing. This is a conversation about sanctification, not justification. As we've studied previously, we're justified by faith alone in what God did for us through Jesus Christ. However, sanctification is when we cooperate with God's Holy Spirit in transforming us from the inside out. Therefore, Paul's teaching about seeds that go into the ground and grow is an excellent illustration with rich, relevant application to our lives.

Read Galatians 6:7-8. We will always reap what we

_____.

When we live to satisfy our sinful nature, we harvest

_____.

When we live by the Holy Spirit, we harvest

_____.

Why do we think that planting bad attitudes or ungodly behaviors will reap good things in the end? God's Holy Spirit won't produce what we won't plant. This reflects Paul's previous conversation about license, or the attitude that we can do whatever we want when we want to do it. Sowing and reaping remind us that our actions are never isolated in a moment; there are long-term, even generational, consequences to our faithfulness as well as to our sinful behavior.

In Matthew 13:3-23, Jesus teaches about different kinds of sowing and reaping. Then, in the verses that follow, he teaches a more sobering lesson—one that the Galatians also would have related to on a deep level.

Read Matthew 13:24-30 and mark the following T (true) or F (false).

____ 1. The man planted good seeds in his field. (v. 24)

____ 2. The enemy came and planted good seeds while everyone was asleep. (v. 25)

_____ 3. Both wheat and weeds began to grow at the same time. (v. 26)

_____ 4. The man knew who had planted the weeds. (v. 28)

_____ 5. He sent out his servants to pull out the weeds. (v. 29)

_____ 6. The weeds will be pulled and burned when the wheat is gathered. (v. 30)

Just as Paul's audience would have known the life-and-death nature of sowing and reaping, Jesus's audience would have been familiar with it as well. So, when Jesus told this story about the good and bad seeds, I imagine his audience's eyes might have widened with surprise, because any good farmer would have plucked out the weeds as soon as they were seen. The weeds in Jesus's story, then, were likely tares, which were a rye grass with poisonous seeds. The difficulty with tares is that they look like wheat until they're fully grown at harvest and are revealed to be destructive.[8]

Jesus's parable highlights three important lessons that Paul taught the Galatians, and these lessons are sobering reminders for us today:

1. Many who teach in Jesus's name are not teaching the gospel.
2. There's always a delay between sowing and reaping, but God won't forget to deal justly with false teachers when the time comes.
3. Our job is to focus on our own growth and not be influenced by the poisonous seeds that false teachers try to spread.

It's frustrating when we see and hear teachers falsely teaching or representing the gospel. Why do you think God allows this? (There's no wrong answer here; just share your thoughts.)

If you've ever planned a garden, you know that whatever kind of seeds you put into the soil will grow. When you plant carrot seeds, you're going to get carrots, not onions. Onions will never grow from carrots. The same is true spiritually. The fruit of the Spirit will never grow from works of the flesh. As we learn from Paul about how our freedom in Christ impacts our relationships with others, we need to recognize that our relationships are influenced by what we plant.

Reaping and Relationships Exercise

Reflect on three relationships in your life, writing each in the diagram below:

1. A satisfying relationship
2. A challenging relationship
3. A new relationship

On the top two lines, list what you've planted in each relationship. On the bottom three lines, write words that reflect what you have reaped from the relationship. (*The Word Bank in the margin offers some suggestions.*)

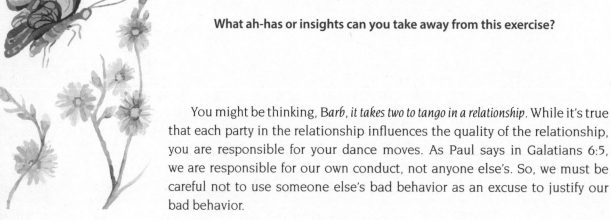

Relationship #1
Seeds Planted

Relationship #2
Seeds Planted

Relationship #3
Seeds Planted

Harvest Reaped

Harvest Reaped

Harvest Reaped

What ah-has or insights can you take away from this exercise?

You might be thinking, *Barb, it takes two to tango in a relationship*. While it's true that each party in the relationship influences the quality of the relationship, you are responsible for your dance moves. As Paul says in Galatians 6:5, we are responsible for our own conduct, not anyone else's. So, we must be careful not to use someone else's bad behavior as an excuse to justify our bad behavior.

I began attending a support group because I wanted to find tips and solutions to change the person in my life who was struggling with addiction. While I didn't cause the issue, I couldn't change it or cure it either. Yet, my response was my responsibility. As I began to self-reflect, the Holy Spirit opened my eyes to the harvest of anger, bitterness, and fear that came from the words, attitudes, and actions I had freely planted on my own. That breakthrough moment in my life revealed a lot of pain and ugly pride that I needed to surrender. But it was necessary in order for me to repent and commit to allowing the Holy Spirit to plant new seeds in me.

It took time for those new seeds to take root and multiply, but they did as I allowed the Spirit to keep working in my life. While the other person didn't change, what I contributed to the relationship did.

Write Galatians 6:9 below:

Why do you think doing good can be so tiring?

What is the outcome of doing good, if we keep going?

The Greek word for "good" is *kalos*, which means "attractive, inspires, motivates."[9] Of course, we want to produce that kind of outcome for God. Yet, it's really easy to shift from Spirit-led production into self-generated production. We cannot do God's good work on our own without God's power; if we try, we'll only burn out.

Have you ever burned out trying to do good things for God? If so, describe it briefly:

As you reflect on that experience, what are some factors that led to you getting burned out?

As one who experienced spiritual burnout years ago, I had a few "lightbulb" breakthrough moments on my long road back to spiritual and emotional wellness. First, God can work powerfully in what doesn't get done just as He works in what does get done. Much of my burnout came from believing that God liked it when I worked long hours beyond my physical strength or available time. However, a second "lightbulb" breakthrough moment was realizing that God never called me to sacrifice my health or my relationships by spending too much time and energy serving Him. This breakthrough taught me that there will always be more requests and opportunities than the time and energy I have available.

Additionally, I learned to honor my body and how it is feeling as well as my most important relationships. It's always hard to say no, but part of finding my freedom in Christ has meant learning not to tie my self-esteem or self-worth to my performance, my ministry position, or others' approval.

Here's the question I ask myself to prevent burnout: *What are the things that only I can do?*

Most of us love being asked! Whether we're being asked to join a Bible study, lead a group, give a message, or chair a committee, it feels good to be asked. Yet, I've learned that there's a difference between the thrill of being asked and the wisdom of knowing whether to accept.

God's Holy Spirit has gifted each believer with spiritual gifts for the purpose of serving the church. Part of my burnout-avoidance maintenance plan is remembering that I am not gifted to do everything. Neither are you! We're given different gifts so that we need each other and serve each other.

Therefore, when I am asked to speak, write, or join something exciting, I need to consider whether I'm called to use my Spirit-enabled gifts and abilities or whether someone else is a better fit for that spot. That's scary if my self-esteem or self-worth is attached to feeling needed. But it's a reflection of my beautiful freedom in Christ when I can say, "Thank you for that invitation. Based on what you've shared with me, I could do this; but I think that there is another woman who is uniquely gifted for this task, and I don't want to stand in her spot."

I've used that response many times over the years. It has been fun watching God use other women so powerfully when I am willing to get out of the way. Personally, it also has allowed me to remain focused on what God has called me to do in His strength and power.

Take a moment to reflect on my two breakthrough moments regarding burnout:

1. **God can work powerfully in what doesn't get done just as He works in what does get done.**
2. **God never called me to sacrifice my health or my relationships by spending too much time and energy serving Him.**

What are your thoughts? Are there any ah-ha moments for you?

Ah-ha Moment

Did you notice any ah-ha spiritual breakthrough moments in today's study, your prayer time, or your daily activities? If so, record that moment on the final page of this week's study (page 201).

If you are battling spiritual burnout today, trust that God sees you and loves you. I pray that you give yourself permission to receive God's love, power, and renewing strength in this season.

Prayer

Dear God, I want to sow the fruit of the Spirit in each of my relationships so that I can be a blessing to others. You know how tough my relationship is with _____. God, I desire for all of the fruit of the Spirit to bloom within me, especially (insert a specific attribute of the fruit of the Spirit) _____. Thank You, Lord, for hearing my prayer; in Jesus's name. Amen.

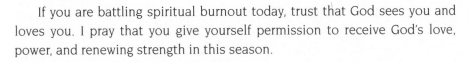

Day 4: What Counts Most

In the Bible, what do the woman caught in adultery, the unnamed bleeding woman, the woman at the well, and the immoral woman at Simon's house have in common? These nameless women met Jesus in difficult if not impossible situations, and he changed their lives. While you may not know each of their stories, these women have two things in common. First, Jesus saved them. Second, they didn't have to do anything to earn it.

I've always wondered why these women weren't named, especially since Jesus had such a big impact on their lives. After all, the circumstances of these women were notorious, so the different gospel authors could have approached them or asked someone for their name. Yet, it's in their nameless

Big Idea

Being changed from the inside out matters most!

state that I can see myself in their story. While I can't relate to their specific circumstances, I can join in their celebration because, like them, Jesus saved me from an impossible situation—my sinful state. His grace changed my life, and I didn't have to do anything to earn it.

There's something so freeing and joyful about not being responsible for earning or maintaining my own salvation. Furthermore, there's the promise of wholeness and peace as the Holy Spirit continues the work that God began when He saved me. That promise of wholeness and peace is for you too. Our time together may be coming to an end, but the Holy Spirit's work continues, which means that your spiritual breakthroughs will continue as well.

I hope that as you've journeyed through the *Breakthrough* study, you've come to fully realize the power of the gospel. During our first week, I introduced the Gospel Wheel and the Legalism Wheel. The Gospel Wheel captures the activity of God's perfect promises in our lives that lead us to spiritual freedom. The Legalism Wheel demonstrates a never-satisfying hamster wheel of To-Do, Do-More, and Do-Better hoops that keep us enslaved in legalism.

Let's revisit the Gospel Wheel and Legalism Wheel. As you reflect on your life right now, answer the questions below the graphic:

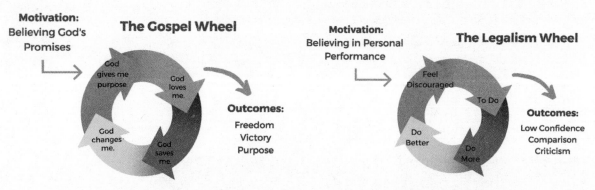

1. **Which wheel are you moving in more often these days? Explain your response.**

2. **Each wheel spins on the momentum of either believing God's promises or believing in your personal performance. What are some of God's promises that you need to be more intentional in believing and clinging to for your life?**

3 Look at the outcomes associated with each wheel. Which ones have you experienced lately? What parts of the wheel do you associate with those outcomes? (For example: Victory might be associated with "God changes me" and Comparison might be associated with "Do More.")

4. As you reflect on the two wheels, what are your takeaways?

As we discussed at the beginning of this week's study, the point of living by the Spirit is not so that you can prove you're more spiritual than others. Clearly, that's a legalistic trap. God gives us the Holy Spirit to transform our hearts so that we can love God and others better, not show off our spiritually. The goal of sanctification isn't to give us a degree in "holier-than-thou" living, impress others, or prove that we're super spiritual. The goal is for us to love others and live our lives like Jesus—in obedience, purpose, and service. I love the following story that illustrates this well:

> A woman . . . came up to her pastor and said, "Pastor, we need to see more signs and wonders. We just haven't seen enough signs and wonders." The pastor responded, "Ma'am, over there sits a lady who has been evicted from her apartment with her children. I would consider it a sign and wonder if you would take them into your house to live for three months."[10]

Because the Holy Spirit is at work in the life of every believer, our faith communities should be places where we're all cooperating with the Spirit's leadings. When we visualize the outcomes of the Gospel Wheel, our life together should be marked by stories of freedom, victory, purpose, and security.

Look at Galatians 6:10 in the margin. Of all of the relationships impacted by our Spirit-led life, which relationships should benefit most from the Spirit's work within us?

Therefore, whenever we have the opportunity, we should do good to everyone—especially to those in the family of faith.
(Galatians 6:10)

If you're wondering what "doing good" looks like, the New Testament contains a litany of statements that give practical wisdom on how to bless each other in the body of Christ.

Look up each Scripture and write beside it how we are to love and take care of one another:

Mark 9:50

James 5:9

Romans 12:10

Ephesians 4:2

Colossians 3:13

James 4:11

Some of us have some pretty tough memories associated with the people in our communities of faith. As we've discussed, church hurt happens. I don't want to diminish any insensitive comments, judgmental attitudes, manipulation, or abuse that you or someone you know may have experienced through a church or someone in church leadership.

As one who has experienced church hurt in many different forms, Galatians 6:10 can be a challenge for me. Here are five lessons from this verse that we cannot neglect if we are going to be led by God's Spirit and walk in freedom:

1. Our freedom in Christ cannot be shaken or taken away by another believer's choice to not live like Christ.
2. The power of the gospel is greater than the imperfect people in our churches.
3. When church hurt happens, we can follow the footprint of God's promises for our lives.
4. Since unity is at the heart of Spirit-led community, we cannot withdraw from church permanently; however, we don't need anyone's permission to leave a specific unhealthy, legalistic church environment.
5. Doing good to other believers isn't an option; it's a Spirit-led obligation.

Do any of these statements have personal application to what you have been through or are going through now? If so, how?

When we do good toward one another as believers, our community benefits and our collective lights shine brighter for Christ. Just as the early church in Acts 2 took care of one another and God added to their community, when we take care of each other as believers, then nonbelievers will notice and want to know more. Doing good isn't always easy, especially when we have different personalities and preferences; but when we ask the Holy Spirit for help, it's possible!

Read Galatians 6:11. What does Paul draw attention to here?

In ancient times, scribes were commonly employed to write for teachers and scholars. By drawing attention to the size of the handwriting in the final lines of his letter, Paul was making a comparison to the presumably smaller handwriting of the rest of the letter as a way of emphasizing that the letter was genuine. His decision to script in his own handwriting was a way of adding emphasis or authority, much like a celebrity handwriting a personal letter instead of assigning the task to an assistant. This personalization would have increased the intimacy and connection between Paul and the church that he almost died to plant. And whether or not it was his intent, perhaps Paul's own handwriting served to highlight his final remarks.

Paul makes one final plea to the Galatians, reminding them of the Judaizers' true motivations and contrasting his attitude with theirs.

Read Galatians 6:12-15.

What are the Judaizers' two motivations for teaching circumcision? (v. 12)

They want to i_____ others.

They want to avoid p_____.

What do the Judaizers boast about? (v. 13)

What does Paul say that he boasts about? (v. 14)

Ah-ha Moment

Did you notice any ah-ha spiritual breakthrough moments in today's study, your prayer time, or your daily activities? If so, record that moment on the final page of this week's study (page 201).

At the heart of legalism is the desire to seek credit for doing what God has already done. Instead of relying on grace, we might leverage To-Do actions in order to earn God's favor or use Do-More behaviors in order to prove to God that you're a good Christian. There's a part inside of us that shouts, "Look at what I've done!" whenever we have a legalistic moment worth celebrating.

Yet Paul gives up his personal celebration, and his proclamation sounds like, "Look at what God has done!" Paul doesn't have to declare his transformation because the Spirit's work within Paul is evident for everyone to see.

The same is true for you and me. When the Spirit is at work in our lives, people will notice; and our response can be, "Look what God has done!"

Prayer

Dear God, thank You for what You've done in my life! Thank You for my freedom in Christ and for bringing me victory, purpose, and security through Your promises. God, as I deal with some of the problems I have with other Christians, remind me to be intentional about doing good as well as being wise in my interactions with those whose lives influence mine; in Jesus's name. Amen.

Day 5: Beyond Breakthrough

Big Idea

Our freedom in Christ is a gift that keeps giving!

Today is the last lesson in our *Breakthrough* journey together. However, I pray that the seeds of time, sacrifice, prayer, and obedience continue to yield spiritual breakthroughs in your life on a regular basis!

As I write this last day of study, I'm celebrating my youngest daughter's birthday. Earlier in the day, we ate lunch on a blanket overlooking the river. As I looked out on the water, a few boats passed by. I noticed that the boats had engines to propel them over the moving water toward whatever the desired location might be. I didn't see anyone paddling in those boats. Why? Because they had an engine to get the job done.

That scene reminded me of the difference between trusting God's promises to lead me to freedom in Christ versus relying on my own limited human performance. Like that engine, God's promises provide power far more effective than anything I could do. But, if I begin comparing myself to other Christians or listening to false voices, essentially I will be pulling out my own spiritual paddles. Not only will I find myself exhausted from the constant "spiritual paddling" as described by those To-Do, Do-More, and Do-Better religious hoops, but I also will completely miss the freedom to ride along on God's adventure of faith for me.

I don't want you to miss the adventure either. Beyond each of your spiritual breakthroughs is a greater expression of your freedom in Christ. As you live free from To-Do, Do-More, and Do-Better hoops and flow in the Gospel Wheel's cycle of freedom, victory, and purpose, you'll discover where and how the Spirit is leading you to live and love others better. Perhaps it's right in your own home by loving your family without imposing legalistic rules on them. Maybe it's an opportunity to lead a Bible study or other ministry team, nurturing other believers. Whatever you are led to do, your freedom in Christ will be a light that shines for God's glory!

In light of all that you've learned, describe what it would look like for you to live fully in your freedom in Christ:

As we wrap up our study today, we're going to take a quick look at Paul's final words to the Galatians, which are fitting for our final time together.

Read Galatians 6:16-18 and answer the following questions.

Paul prays for God's _____ **and** _____
for those who've been transformed by Christ. (v. 16)

What does Paul have on his body as evidence of his faith in Christ? (v. 17)

Paul prays that the Galatians experience the
_____ **of Jesus Christ in their spirits. (v. 18)**

Paul wraps up his letter to the Galatians with a blessing, a reminder, and then another blessing. In verse 16, he prays for God's peace and mercy. This prayer aligns with God's promises for His children. Jesus promises us peace in John 16:33, and in Hebrews 4:16 we are promised mercy when we approach God for help.

In verse 17, Paul's attitude seems a little spicy one last time! His body bears the literal scars of his faith. We've read about the troubles he experienced when planting the churches in Galatia, and he endured other imprisonments and punishments as well (2 Corinthians 11:24-31). The legalists, by contrast, didn't bear any scars that resulted because of their faith in Christ, though they did endure brief pain for the law of circumcision.

Finally, in verse 18, Paul prays grace or wholeness in Christ over the believers. For all of his passionate, sometimes pointed teaching, Paul loved the Galatians and wanted them to live in freedom.

That's my prayer for you as well. This study has covered some tender topics such as legalism, church hurt, toxic Christianity, slavery, race, and more. I want to commend you for investing your time in this study, including the time you've spent with others if you did this study with a group. As we bring things to a close, take a moment to reflect on all you've learned from your study of Galatians.

What are three takeaways, verses, or stories from the Letter to the Galatians that you want to remember? (You might want to flip through your workbook or the Letter to the Galatians in your Bible.)

1.

2.

3.

Now, before our final prayer together, spend some time thinking about your spiritual breakthroughs—those you've experienced this week as well as those from previous weeks.

Weekly Breakthrough Reflection Exercise

Each day this week you have been prompted to record on this page any ah-ha spiritual breakthrough moments you've had in your study, prayer time, or daily activities. Take time now to reflect once more on where you've seen God working in your heart, mind, and life this week, and add any other ah-ha moments below.

Lightbulb
You gain new understanding about God or yourself.

Describe the moment:

_____

_____

_____

Butterfly
You surrender or let go of a struggle, sin, or stronghold from your past.

Describe the moment:

_____

_____

_____

Rainbow
You find new or renewed hope based on God's promises for your life.

Describe the moment:

_____

_____

_____

Busted Brick Wall
You confront and face up to any kind of fear or worry.

Describe the moment:

_____

_____

_____

Line in the Sand
You realize that a sin, struggle, or stronghold is no longer acceptable.

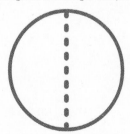

Describe the moment:

_____

_____

_____

Split-the-Rock
You have a supernatural shift in your faith or circumstances after faithfully praying and letting God lead.

Describe the moment:

_____

_____

_____

Now, review all of the Weekly Breakthrough Reflection Exercises at the end of each week, and take a moment to celebrate the different breakthroughs you have experienced throughout this study.

As you consider all of the spiritual breakthroughs you've recorded, are there any that stand out to you? Are some more surprising than others? Write your thoughts below:

Where do you still need God's freedom in your life?

A Final Blessing

It may be the end of our time together, but it's the beginning of the next chapter in your journey of freedom in Christ. I want to leave you with a final blessing. While I may not have been with you physically each day as you worked through this Bible study, I've been praying with you and for you. My dream is that after you complete this lesson and close this workbook, you will continue to grow in your freedom in Christ.

This blessing is a prayer that you can come back to whenever you seem to be spinning around the Legalism Wheel of To-Do, Do-More, and Do-Better—or feeling you're not good enough for God. If you want, you can remove the page and post it somewhere you can read it as needed. You can read it as written as my blessing over you, or feel free to personalize it, using first-person language.

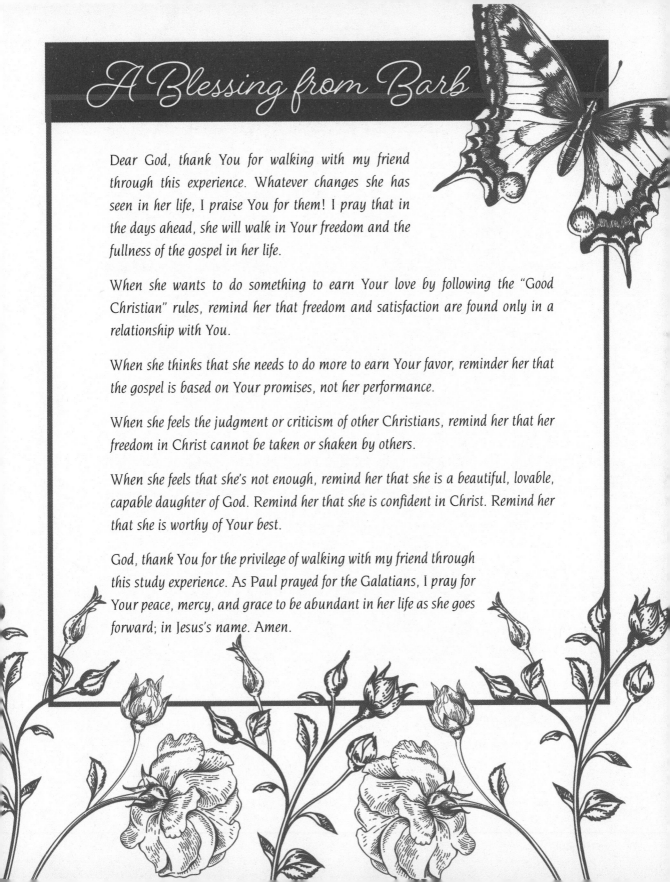

A Blessing from Barb

Dear God, thank You for walking with my friend through this experience. Whatever changes she has seen in her life, I praise You for them! I pray that in the days ahead, she will walk in Your freedom and the fullness of the gospel in her life.

When she wants to do something to earn Your love by following the "Good Christian" rules, remind her that freedom and satisfaction are found only in a relationship with You.

When she thinks that she needs to do more to earn Your favor, reminder her that the gospel is based on Your promises, not her performance.

When she feels the judgment or criticism of other Christians, remind her that her freedom in Christ cannot be taken or shaken by others.

When she feels that she's not enough, remind her that she is a beautiful, lovable, capable daughter of God. Remind her that she is confident in Christ. Remind her that she is worthy of Your best.

God, thank You for the privilege of walking with my friend through this study experience. As Paul prayed for the Galatians, I pray for Your peace, mercy, and grace to be abundant in her life as she goes forward; in Jesus's name. Amen.

Video Viewer Guide
WEEK 6

Scriptures: Galatians 6:9-10, Matthew 5:14-16, Galatians 6:14-16

Take time to _____ and _____ your spiritual breakthroughs and God's work in your life.

Tell others about your breakthroughs to give _____ to God.

Freedom Principle Review

1. The gospel of grace is based on God's perfect promises, not our performance.

2. A relationship with God means that we receive from Him rather than follow rules for Him.

3. Your freedom in Christ can't be shaken or taken away by someone's choice not to live like Christ.

4. Freedom in Christ is living free from fear and fully alive with joy and purpose.

5. Spiritual breakthrough is an ah-ha moment when we recognize that God is at work within us, receive what He's doing, and respond to it.

Freedom Principle #6

You are God's beautiful, lovable, capable daughter.

You are _____ in Christ

and _____ of God's best.

Notes

Biblical Background on Galatians

1. David Guzik, "Challenging a Different Gospel," Study Guide for Galatians 1, https://www.blueletterbible.org/Comm /guzik_david/StudyGuide2017-Gal/Gal-1.cfm?a=1092005.
2. Clinton E. Arnold, gen. ed., *Exegetical Commentary on the New Testament: Galatians* (Grand Rapids, MI: Zondervan, 2010), 23.
3. Arnold, gen. ed., *Exegetical Commentary on the New Testament: Galatians*, 23.
4. Arnold, gen. ed., *Exegetical Commentary on the New Testament: Galatians*, 27.
5. Arnold, gen. ed., *Exegetical Commentary on the New Testament: Galatians*, 23.
6. Arnold, gen. ed., *Exegetical Commentary on the New Testament: Galatians*, 26.
7. Arnold, gen. ed., *Exegetical Commentary on the New Testament: Galatians*, 29.

Week 1

1. Warren Wiersbe, *The Wiersbe Bible Commentary: New Testament* (Colorado Springs: David C. Cook, 2007), 149.
2. Ronald F. Youngblood, *Nelson's Illustrated Bible Dictionary: New and Enhanced Edition* (Nashville: Thomas Nelson, 2014), 1135.
3. Youngblood, *Nelson's Illustrated Bible Dictionary*, 82-83.
4. Tim Keller, *Galatians for You* (Epson, Surrey, England: The Good Book Company, 2012), 14.
5. AlleyDog, s.v. "curse of knowledge," https://www.alleydog.com/glossary/definition.php?term=Curse+Of+Knowledge.
6. Bible Hub, s.v. "charis," https://biblehub.com/greek/5485.htm.
7. Bible Hub, s.v. "eirene," https://biblehub.com/greek/1515.htm.

8. David Guzik, "Galatians 1 – Challenging a Different Gospel," Study Guide for Galatians 1, https://www.blueletterbible.org/Comm/guzik_david/StudyGuide2017-Gal/Gal-1.cfm?a=1092005.
9. Philip Yancey, *What's So Amazing about Grace?* (Nashville: Harper Collins, 1997), 55.
10. Jerry Bridges, *The Discipline of Grace: God's Role and Our Role in the Pursuit of Holiness* (Colorado Springs: NavPress, 2006), 19.
11. David Platt and Tony Merida, *Exalting Jesus in Galatians: Christ-Centered Exposition Commentary* (Nashville: B&H Publishing, 2014), 9.
12. Bible Hub, s.v. "euaggelion," https://biblehub.com/str/greek/2098.htm.
13. Tracy Munsil, "AWVI 2020 Survey: 1 in 3 US Adults Embrace Salvation Through Jesus; More Believe It Can Be 'Earned,'" Cultural Research Center, Arizona Christian University, https://www.arizonachristian.edu/blog/2020/08/04/1-in-3-us-adults-embrace-salvation-through-jesus-more-believe-it-can-be-earned/
14. *Merriam-Webster*, s.v. "adventure," https://www.merriam-webster.com/dictionary/adventure.
15. Platt and Merida, *Exalting Jesus in Galatians*, 9.
16. Platt and Merida, *Exalting Jesus in Galatians*, 10.
17. Warren Wiersbe, *The Wiersbe Bible Commentary*, 548.
18. Youngblood, *Nelson's Illustrated Bible Dictionary*, 641.
19. Clinton E. Arnold, gen ed,. *Zondervan Illustrated Bible Backgrounds Commentary*, Volume 2: John, Acts (Grand Rapids: Zondervan, 2002), 138.
20. Tony Evans, *The Tony Evans Bible Commentary* (Nashville: Holman Bible Publishers, 2019), 1092.
21. Arnold, gen. ed., *Exegetical Commentary on the New Testament: Galatians*, 41.
22. Platt and Merida, *Exalting Jesus in Galatians*, 6.
23. Tracy Munsil, "AWVI 2020 Survey: 1 in 3 US Adults Embrace Salvation Through Jesus; More Believe It Can Be 'Earned,'" Cultural Research Center, Arizona Christian University, August 4, 2020, https://www.arizonachristian.edu/blog/2020/08/04/1-in-3-us-adults-embrace-salvation-through-jesus-more-believe-it-can-be-earned/
24. Warren Wiersbe, *Be Free: Exchange Legalism for True Spirituality* (Colorado Springs, CO: David C. Cook, 1975), 11.
25. Wiersbe, *The Weirsbe Bible Commentary: New Testament*, 548.
26. Wiersbe, *The Weirsbe Bible Commentary: New Testament*, 548.
27. Ferris Jabr, "How Does a Caterpillar Turn Into a Butterfly?" *Scientific American*, August 10, 2012, https://www.scientificamerican.com/article/caterpillar-butterfly-metamorphosis-explainer/#:~:text=One%20day%2C%20the%20caterpillar%20stops,as%20a%20butterfly%20or%20moth.
28. "Zacchaeus," Biblical Training, https://www.biblicaltraining.org/library/zacchaeus.
29. Wiersbe, *The Weirsbe Bible Commentary: New Testament*, 202.

Week 2

1. "Early Church," The Bible Timeline, http://www.biblehistory.com/period/early-church.
2. Clinton E. Arnold, gen ed,. *Zondervan Illustrated Bible Backgrounds Commentary*, Volume 2: John, Acts, 333.

3. Clinton E. Arnold, gen. ed, *Exegetical Commentary on the New Testament: Galatians*, 31.

4. Arnold, *Exegetical Commentary on the New Testament: Galatians*, 26.

5. "Important Events in Church History: Christian History Timeline," Christian History, https://www.christianitytoday.com/history/issues/issue-28/important-events-in-church-history-christian-history.html.

6. Youngblood, *Nelson's Illustrated Bible Dictionary*, 1139.

7. Keller, *Galatians for You*, 40.

8. Keller, *Galatians for You*, 38.

9. Youngblood, *Nelson's Illustrated Bible Dictionary*, 275.

10. Wiersbe, *The Wiersbe Bible Commentary: New Testament*, 593.

11. Platt and Merida, *Exalting Jesus in Galatians*, 40.

12. Arnold, gen. ed., *Exegetical Commentary on the New Testament: Galatians*, 273.

13. Youngblood, *Nelson's Illustrated Bible Dictionary*, 1149.

14. Hope Bolinger, "What Is the Torah?" Christianity.com, https://www.christianity.com/wiki/bible/what-is-the-torah.html.

15. Youngblood, *Nelson's Illustrated Bible Dictionary*, 1149.

16. Youngblood, *Nelson's Illustrated Bible Dictionary*, 1149.

17. Youngblood, *Nelson's Illustrated Bible Dictionary*, 673–74.

18. Evans, *The Tony Evans Bible Commentary*, 1323.

19. "The Covenants," BibleProject, https://bibleproject.com/explore/covenants/.

20. Evans, *The Tony Evans Bible Commentary*, 1167.

21. Wiersbe, *The Wiersbe Bible Commentary: New Testament*, 21.

22. Josh McDowell and Don Stewart, *Answers to Tough Questions Skeptics Ask About the Christian Faith* (San Bernardino: Here's Life Publishers, 1980), 128.

23. Josh McDowell, "Why Should I Become a Christian? The Worst Hypocrites Are in the Church," Josh McDowell Ministry, https://www.josh.org/resources/apologetics/answering-skeptics-detail/.

24. Robert Velarde, "What About Hypocrites in the Church?" Focus on the Family, January 1, 2009, https://www.focusonthefamily.com/faith/what-about-hypocrites-in-the-church/.

25. Bible Hub, s.v., "antihistémi," https://biblehub.com/greek/436.htm.

26. Platt and Merida, *Exalting Jesus in Galatians*, 41.

27. Evans, *The Tony Evans Bible Commentary*, 1203.

28. Wiersbe, *The Wiersbe Bible Commentary: New Testament*, 555.

29. Evans, *The Tony Evans Bible Commentary*, 1203

30. Arnold, gen. ed., *Exegetical Commentary on the New Testament: Galatians*, 151.

31. Arnold, gen. ed., *Exegetical Commentary on the New Testament: Galatians*, 155.

32. Guy Waters, "What Are Justification and Sanctification?" Ligonier Ministries, https://www.ligonier.org/learn/articles/what-are-justification-and-sanctification/.

33. Andy Crouch, Afterward to *UnChristian: What a New Generation Really Thinks about Christianity . . . and Why It Matters*, by David Kinnaman and Gabe Lyons (Grand Rapids, MI: Baker, 2007), 230.

34. James Harleman, "The Avengers: Red in your Ledger," Cinemagogue, May 14, 2012 , http://cinemagogue.com/2012/05/14/the-avengers-red-in-your-ledger/.

35. Arnold, gen. ed., *Exegetical Commentary on the New Testament: Galatians*, 166.

36. Keller, *Galatians for You*, 60.

37. Keller, *Galatians for You*, 62.

Week 3

1. Bible Hub, s.v. "anoétos," https://biblehub.com/greek/453.htm.

2. Keller, *Galatians for You*, 83.

3. Tony Evans, *The Tony Evans Bible Commentary*, 1205.

4. Platt and Merida, *Exalting Jesus in Galatians*, 56.

5. Evans, *The Tony Evans Bible Commentary*, 70.

6. E. Ray Clendenen and Jeremy Royal, eds., "Genesis 15:17," *Holman Illustrated Bible Commentary* (Nashville: B&H Publshing Group, 2015), 29.

7. Keller, *Galatians for You*, 60.

8. Lisa Bevere, *You Are Not What You Weigh: End Your War With Food and Discover Your True Value* (United Kingdom: Charisma House, 2013), 2.

9. Elizabeth Nix, "What Is Juneteenth?" History, last updated June 18, 2020, https://www.history.com/news/what-is-juneteenth

10. Bible Hub, s.v. "paidagógos," https://biblehub.com/greek/3807.htm.

11. Clint Arnold, gen. ed., *Zondervan Illustrated Bible Backgrounds Commentary: Romans to Philemon* (Grand Rapids: Zondervan, 2002), 284.

12. Arnold, *Zondervan Illustrated Bible Backgrounds Commentary*, 284.

13. Keller, *Galatians for You*, 92.

14. Clinton Arnold, gen ed., *Zondervan Exegetical Commentary on the New Testament: Galatians*, 260.

15. Tony Evans, *Let's Get to Know Each Other: What White and Black Christians Need to Know About Each Other* (Nashville: Thomas Nelson, Inc., 1995), 130.

16. Matt Perman, "What Is the Doctrine of the Trinity?" Desiring God, January 26, 2006, https://www.desiringgod.org/articles/what-is-the-doctrine-of-the-trinity.

17. Youngblood, *Nelson's Illustrated Bible Dictionary*, 1157.

18. Evans, *The Tony Evans Bible Commentary*, 59.

19. Weirsbe, *The Weirsbe Bible Commentary: Old Testament*, 52.

20. Theodore Hiebert, *The Beginning of Difference: Discovering Identity in God's Diverse World* (Nashville: Abingdon Press, 2019), 51.

21. Martin Luther King, Jr., speech at Western Michigan University, December 18, 1963, https://wmich.edu/sites/default/files/attachments/MLK.pdf, 22.

22. Teesha Hadra and John Hambrick, *Black and White: Disrupting Racism One Friendship at a Time* (Nashville: Abingdon Press, 2019), 17–18.

Week 4

1. Youngblood, *Nelson's Illustrated Bible Dictionary*, 1073.

2. Walter Scheidel, "The Roman Slave Supply," Stanford University, 2007, https://www.princeton.edu/~pswpc/pdfs/scheidel/050704.pdf.

3. "Slaves and Freemen," PBS, https://www.pbs.org/empires/romans/empire/slaves_freemen.html.

4. Youngblood, *Nelson's Illustrated Bible Dictionary*, 1074.
5. Wiersbe, *Be Free*, 93.
6. Platt and Merida, *Exalting Jesus in Galatians*, 74.
7. Platt and Merida, *Exalting Jesus in Galatians*, 69.
8. Wiersbe, *The Wiersbe Bible Commentary: New Testament*, 565.
9. Evans, *The Tony Evans Commentary*, 160.
10. Platt and Merida, *Exalting Jesus in Galatians*, 81.
11. Youngblood, *Nelson's Illustrated Bible Dictionary*, 536.
12. Keller, *Galatians for You*, 100-101.
13. Wiersbe, *The Wiersbe Bible Commentary: New Testament*, 565.
14. Wiersbe, *Be Free*, 97.
15. Platt and Merida, *Exalting Jesus in Galatians*, 89.
16. Barb Roose, *I'm Waiting, God: Finding Blessing in God's Delays* (Nashville: Abingdon Press, 2019) 28.
17. "Need a Quick Brain Boost? Take a Walk," Harvard Women's Health Watch, https://www.health.harvard.edu /mind-and-mood/need-a-quick-brain-boost-take-a-walk.

Week 5

1. Donald Alexander, PhD., ed., *Christian Spirituality: Five Views of Sanctification* (Downers Grove: IVP Press, 1989), 13.
2. Wayne Grudem, *Systematic Theology: An Introduction to Bible Doctrine* (Grand Rapids: Zondervan, 1994), 746.
3. Grudem, *Systematic Theology*, 746.
4. Youngblood, *Nelson's Illustrated Bible Dictionary*, 1148.
5. Platt and Merida, *Exalting Jesus in Galatians*, 101.
6. Barb Roose, *Winning the Worry Battle: Life Lessons from the Book of Joshua* (Nashville: Abingdon Press, 2018), 78.
7. Wiersbe, *The Weirsbe Bible Commentary: New Testament*, 574.
8. E. Ray Clendenen and Jeremy Royal Howard, eds., "Luke 10:33-35," *Holman Illustrated Bible Commentary* (Nashville: B&H Publishing Group, 2015), 1105.
9. Oswald Chambers, *My Utmost for His Highest* (Uhrichsville, OH: Barbour Publishing, 1963), 227.
10. Grace Fox, *My Place for Bible Study: Forever Changed* (Galveston, TX: First Place for Health, 2018), 152.
11. Platt and Merida, *Exalting Jesus in Galatians*, 112.
12. Platt and Merida, *Exalting Jesus in Galatians*, 114.
13. Keller, *Galatians for You*, 153.
14. Penny Noyes, "What are the Fruits of the Spirit?" Christianity.com, https://www.christianity.com/wiki /holy-spirit/what-are-the-fruits-of-the-spirit.html.
15. David Guzik, "Galatians 5: Standing Fast in the Liberty of Jesus," Enduring Word, https://enduringword.com/bible -commentary/galatians-5/.
16. Wiersbe, *The Wiersbe Bible Commentary: New Testament*, 576.
17. Keller, *Galatians for You*, 154.
18. Wiersbe, *The Wiersbe Bible Commentary: New Testament*, 576.
19. Youngblood, *Nelson's Illustrated Bible Dictionary*, 1073.
20. David Guzik, "Galatians 5: Standing Fast in the Liberty of Jesus," Enduring Word, https://enduringword.com/bible -commentary/galatians-5/.
21. Platt and Merida, *Exalting Jesus in Galatians*, 113

22. Clint Arnold, gen. ed., *Zondervan Illustrated Bible Backgrounds Commentary, Volume 3: Romans to Philemon* (Grand Rapids: Zondervan, 2002), 292.
23. Keller, *Galatians for You*, 151.

Week 6

1. Keller, *Galatians for You*, 159.
2. Keller, *Galatians for You*, 167.
3. Clendenen and Howard, eds., *Holman Illustrated Bible Commentary*, 1275.
4. BibleHub.com, s.v. "bastazó," https://biblehub.com/greek /941.htm.
5. Clendenen and Howard, eds., *Holman Illustrated Bible Commentary*, 1275.
6. Keller, *Galatians for You*, 168.
7. Eric Ravenscraft, "Why Talking About Our Problems Helps So Much (and How to Do It)," *The New York Times*, https: //www.nytimes.com/2020/04/03/smarter-living/talking-out -problems.html.
8. Arnold, gen. ed., *Zondervan Illustrated Bible Backgrounds Commentary, Volume 1: Matthew, Mark, Luke* (Grand Rapids: Zondervan, 2002), 85-86.
9. Bible Hub, s.v. "kalos," https://biblehub.com/greek/2570.htm.
10. Platt and Merida, *Exalting Jesus in Galatians*, 120

Video Viewer Guide
ANSWERS

Week 1
past / problems / pain
receiving / rules
To Do
Do More
Do Better
recognize / receive / respond
promises / performance

Week 2
mistakes
repents / resists
eyes
receive / rules

Week 3
transforms
transmits
transcends
shaken / taken

Week 4
released / reassigned
rules / free
power / presence
fear

Week 5
free / pressuring
practice / perfection
transformed
recognize / receive / respond

Week 6
acknowledge / celebrate
glory
confident / worthy